EDGAR ALLAN POE
PUZZLES
CONUNDRUMS OF MYSTERY AND IMAGINATION

DR GARETH MOORE

SIRIUS

SIRIUS

This edition published in 2023 by Sirius Publishing, a division of
Arcturus Publishing Limited,
26/27 Bickels Yard, 151–153 Bermondsey Street,
London SE1 3HA

ISBN: 978-1-3988-0920-8
AD008310NT

Printed in China

CONTENTS

INTRODUCTION

Dear Reader,

There is much to question in this world of shadows. As I pass through these diminishing days I find myself troubled. Figures move at the edges of my vision, yet vanish in the full glare of my gaze, while screeches of nocturnal birds haunt my sleep from some distant, unearthly realm.

In an effort to dispel the dusky figures that plague my conscience, I set down in these pages a compilation of strange episodes. Each of these mysteries will transport you to places both familiar and uncharted, imagined and actual; places which have imprinted somehow upon my life, my writings, or my unquieted imaginings. Each episode contains within it some manner of confounding conundrum, for solving intricate problems and cryptic ciphers are two joys that can yet cut through the gloom of my spirit's winter to bathe my soul in a sharp, brightened light. And so, I invite you to journey with me through that ethereal barrier into my mind's eye; to push aside the dark boughs of confusion which may block your path, and to unwind as the thread of Ariadne the answers to my many puzzles.

Some of these riddles indulge my preoccupation with language— and in these instances I urge you to keep your wits about you, for sentences are shallow graves from which the smallest details can rise

as ghosts from the page. Remember that all is rarely as it seems: just as dreams conjure dissolving worlds of unmapped wilderness, lost to memory, so words can be artful tricksters. Their meanings can be twisted, leading those who attempt comprehension into misery and ruin. Keep a wary eye for such devious rogues as you venture into these strange tales, for many such confounding meanings can be seen.

But do not rest easy in this knowledge. Some of the incidents I have recounted will call upon your powers of logical reasoning, requiring you to shift the countenance of your perspective. As you gaze through the mists that will rise, cold and forbidding in front of you, remember that the silhouettes which appear may change their shape entirely if viewed from a different angle, or if cast in a different light.

Note also that I have long had a fascination for all methods of encryption; for veiling words and letters in a rippling silk of disguise. With this in mind, you may expect to encounter several pictographs contained within the pages that follow, that conceal like chimera their true meaning behind a façade of familiarity.

As you progress further still, you will also encounter a distinguished character of my own invention, whose ventures in both criminology and detective work will provide many formidable conundrums for you to contemplate. Like his progenitorial author, he is wont to examine the sinister corners of the human spirit, daring to observe what lies within… but no more of this for now, for you shall be introduced to him in full at a later point in this narrative.

Though the crepuscular powers of the supernatural often permeate the words that drape your path, be reassured that all of the information you require to reach the resolution of each problem is provided somewhere within the visible boundaries of each page. It may be cloaked in a miasma of obfuscation, and yet a conclusion may always be achieved through logical thinking and a creative approach. But stay awake, for I cannot promise that when the solutions penetrate your mind that they will not take the shape of forsaken demons to haunt your sleep forever more.

You may journey these challenges of mine in any order you so please, for each tale stands alone, weaving its own curious tapestry. I have of course already wandered the uncertain landscapes they hold, and faced the unsettling shapes which populate them, and so I more than most know the anguish to be found in reckoning with these faceless spirits. Thus if, while wandering through these descriptions, you should find yourself lost and disoriented, or beyond all rescuing through your own mental gifts, you may always find a shortcut via the back pages of the book, where the solution to each enigma is clearly elucidated.

I wish you luck in your exploits, and pray that your meditations will not be disturbed by the tap of a raven at your chamber door.

Edgar Allan Poe

THE FITFUL REST

After falling into fitful slumber late last night, my mind, wheeling from the events of the day, became beset by a most foul nightmare.

Wandering through a desolate forest, my path became blocked by two sallow-faced women, their lace gowns spattered with blood. Both clutched a vial filled with silver liquid, and as I gazed upon them my heart flooded with bitter dread. They extended their arms toward me, and spoke to me with ragged breaths:

"Before you pass, you must drink from one vial. One is poison, the other is not.

"One of us can speak only the truth, while the other only lies. But we will not tell you who is who.

"You may ask us one question."

At this, I awoke, staring at the familiar shapes around me, and found I knew how I would have survived these spectral figures.

Can you work out how to ascertain which of the vials was poison?

AN AMERICAN GARDEN

The house opposite to my own features an ornate garden, with paths which weave through riotous swells of sunflowers, past proud rows of vegetables, and onwards to a secluded bench in the shade of a cypress tree. The plot is lovingly tended each day by an elderly gentleman of solid build, serious countenance, and few words.

One late winter day, as I was returning from a perambulation around the town, he raised his hat to me as he stood by the gate, and uttered a surprising soliloquy:

"I feel quite sure that this is the start of spring and the end of coldness; the beginnings of seasonal sun and the end of winter's sorrows."

I tipped my hat back to him and continued onto my property, but I could not help but note that his utterance had a cryptic truth to it beyond the mere surface reading.

He was describing today, but what else could he have been referring to?

A DIFFERENT TIME

On occasion, I find temporary relief from the tumult of my own thoughts by taking myself back to memories of the dusty corridors of my childhood school.

The ancient solemnity of it! I recall a mathematics teacher, dressed in a faded suit of wool, who upon finding me lost in thought in a gloomy alcove once gave me problems to solve. One of these remains fast in my mind. I do not recall the exact words, but its gist is as follows:

"If $10 + 4 = 2$, and $5 - 6 = 11$, then what does $9 + 7$ equal?"

A WRITER'S APHORISM

I take great pleasure in the cerebral disorientation which comes from the consideration of a well-crafted cipher, and yet more from disentangling an elusive solution. With the aim of widening my expertise and challenging my mind, I advertised in *Alexander's Weekly Messenger* for submissions of such enigmas from the general public to which I could apply myself.

Alas, nothing truly complex has arrived as yet, and this week's offering took me mere seconds to decipher:

"Tahw si yrteop tub yretsym detcelfer?"

What was the message?

FROM THE EDITOR 1: THE HIDDEN TITLE

The weather was foul on one particular Thursday, and I found myself confined to my study with a manuscript that frustrated me beyond measure, with no hope of escape to invigorate my lungs with outside air.

To prevent myself from descending into the familiar fog of despondency, I decided to open a letter from the *Messenger*. It contained, as I had hoped, a submission of a cipher in response to my open request. I quickly ascertained that it was a Caesar shift, a simple cipher through which each letter in a message is moved a constant amount forward or backward through the alphabet. For example, if the shift was forward 3, A would become D, B would become E and so on, with Z becoming C.

I deduced that the message sprawled across the page in a spidery script was the title of a poem by a writer I have often criticized:

DRO KBBYG KXN DRO CYXQ

What was the title?

THE DREAM

The dreams of a writer are all too often beset by a swirling mass of shadow, which may variously condense into disquieting illusions or vaporize into an impenetrable hush. I shall tell you of one such vision which disturbed my sleep.

I stood enveloped in the mist of a dismal afternoon, and though my vision was poor I became aware of a great noose looming above me. My feet began to move irrevocably forward, up the wooden steps one by one, their creaks whispering portents of my impending death.

The executioner stood firm, the guardian of the portal to the accursed flames that lay before me. He looped the rope around my shivering neck and produced a pistol before he spoke.

"You may speak one sentence as I judge your life. If you lie, the noose will be your fate. If you speak the truth, I will shoot you."

At this I swam back into hazy consciousness, finding no relief from the quiet of reality. As I lay, tormented by my mind's own invention, I divined a way to escape both noose and bullet.

What could I have said to perhaps stay the executioner's hand?

WINTER MISFORTUNE

I knew a young man in Baltimore many years ago, with a strange sadness behind his eyes and a tendency to linger a moment longer than is comfortable at the end of a conversation.

I recently had the misfortune to hear of his sorry demise. In the yawning depths of the Baltimore winter, he had been found hanged from the ceiling of his bedroom—but, mysteriously, there was no chair nearby, nor any other surface from which he could have jumped. Indeed, the only unusual thing of note in the room was a small pool of water on the floor.

How did he die?

CIPHER MAIL

U pon opening my correspondence this morning, I discovered a letter from the editor of *Alexander's Weekly Messenger* containing, unsurprisingly, another response to my request for codes and ciphers to solve, which I had submitted to the paper some weeks previously.

The submissions I had received previously had not demonstrated any notable nuance in their disguise, so I did not hold out a great deal of hope. And when I slipped the letter out of its envelope, my suspicions were, unfortunately, confirmed. It read as follows:

AF OU LTEM
PES TAP PR
OACH ES

What ominous prediction has its author attempted to conceal?

THE CIRCUS TENT

I observed the caravans of a circus approaching from the east, curling through the valley like a quiet plume of smoke. The silky panels of a big top were erected, and I resolved to venture forth that same evening to see the show.

Burning torches lit my way as I entered the tent, and the bitter, dry scent of sawdust transported me. My heart quickened at the feats of the acrobats, whose whirling and tumbling made them at times indistinguishable from one another in their serpentine dance.

At length, a magician entered, wearing a black silk hat and a cloak dark enough to wrap my mind in thoughts of unceasing night.

His velvet voice threw the following words into the enclosed space, as he produced a small ball from inside his cloak.

"Welcome, ladies and gentlemen. I have an illusion to present to you, before my humble troupe continue with their performance.

"In a moment, I will throw this ball away from me with all the strength in my body. It will travel for a certain distance, then stop. Then—without any help from me—it will start to move again and fly straight back to my waiting hand.

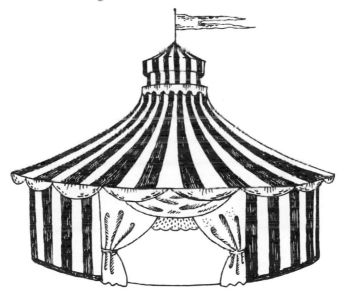

"I promise you, ladies and gentlemen, that no magnets, elastic, strings, or any other element of trickery will be used; only my bare hands will be involved."

I smiled to myself, for I knew how this was to be achieved.

What did the magician do?

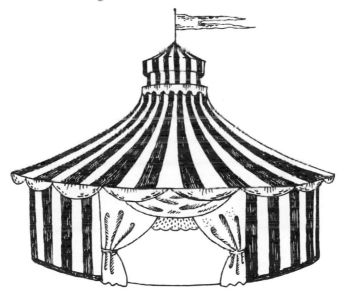

SPECTRAL VISIONS

I am acquainted with a gentleman who recently lost his father to some terrible wasting disease, and is now living alone in the house they once shared. He wrote to me of a most unsettling event which had happened to him some nights previously.

He had been aroused from his bed by a fearful rattling, and in a trance-like state had lit a lamp and advanced toward the sound, feeling the cold clutches of dread begin to tendril around his heart.

What strange lands our own homes seem in the foreign shadows of night, when we have no other living soul to ground us with the comfort of their breathing! He related that as he cast his eyes over the familiar walls of the house, he felt them to be closing in, entombing him in his own unease.

As his terror grew, mysterious images began appearing. Above the twisting leaves carved into the mantlepiece, the spectral contours of his father swam into view, raising his arms to his face in sympathy as the gentleman sought to cast him from view. He stumbled away, only to be faced with the full length of a figure who bore the same features, but was so pale as to seem removed altogether from this world.

At length, the noise had ceased, and he had returned to his bed in a state of fitful exhaustion.

When the watery morning light filtered through the curtains, he considered the night's events but was unable to make sense of such ghostly visions.

I spent some time pondering this conundrum before writing back to him with my deductions. It seemed there could be only one solution that did not involve either delusion or the paranormal.

Where had the images of the man's father come from?

THE SPINSTER'S AMUSEMENT

O n my daily journey to the office of the *Messenger,* a periodical devoted to the literary arts, I would often chance to pass a woman of some ancient age, sitting on her veranda with a tawny cat curled on a chair beside her. Both sets of eyes seemed perpetually alert to my movements, and I always felt a sense of unrest cloud my progress as I passed.

Some days she would call out to me in a cracked voice, that entered my spirit and writhed dismay into my veins.

"Mr. Poe, I hope you have not forgotten how old I am. Hah! I see from your gaze which flickers from mine that you disregard me, and yet here I am in my prime!

"I am past 90, but not yet not 100."

Yet though the sound of her voice chilled my soul, I felt bound to reply.

How old was the woman?

THE TIME OF
THE DEMISE

I am of the belief that there are few humans who are not haunted by thoughts of their own mortality. The mystery of it, the notion that death may come from a chance encounter at an early age, or after many years of suffering in physical decrepitude, holds a dark fascination.

I was once involved in a discussion on this subject with a priest, a man who, despite his intense piety and adherence to the laws prescribed by his church, held a fast certainty in his mind about the time at which his death would occur.

He told me that he was sure that the time of his passing would be at an hour of the day which, if it were two hours later, would be half the amount of time to 6 pm as if it were one hour later.

At what hour of the day did the priest predict that he would die?

A BRISK WALK

As a thin mist descended one evening, I donned my warmest coat and walked out into the cold night air to clear my head of the day's thoughts.

I often find that, on such rambles, I become distracted and then find myself in unfamiliar surroundings—the strangeness of such environments, even in darkness, can perversely bring a twisted comfort.

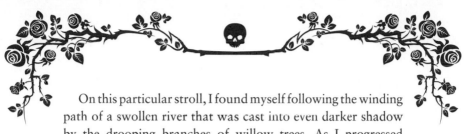

On this particular stroll, I found myself following the winding path of a swollen river that was cast into even darker shadow by the drooping branches of willow trees. As I progressed along the path, I became aware of a man approaching me, similarly clad in a long, dark coat, with a black hat upon his head. Meanwhile, on the other side of the river, I observed his dog, following the man's route from the parallel path on the distant bank.

We passed each other, nodding with the quiet respect of those who walk alone. As he walked away, I heard him call to his hound, who immediately crossed the river to join him, loping away with dry fur. No bridges were in sight, and no boat or ferry had carried the animal across.

How did he cross the river?

THE STATELY LETTER

I received a letter from an old acquaintance that held a distinctly itinerant character:

Dear Mr. Poe,

You may wonder how I have fared since last we spoke. In truth, I spend each day wandering from city to city in search of the place in this great nation which I will one day feel able to call my home.

The most exasperating aspect is how, amid a host of others, I can feel alone; without my own citadel, aware of how unsettled I am. Oh, I only know that over months of exploring I have once more gone too long without sufficient food; I am sinewy, or knifelike in profile. I miss our intellectual conversations, though mostly your domain, even when talking to others.

I plan to visit as many states as is possible in the time I have left. Of course, several have already been crossed off my list. In fact, seven of them are contained within just the

second paragraph of this very letter, which in turn form my
challenge to you. What states are these?

Yours sincerely,
Mr. A D Camore

Which seven US states had Mr. Camore concealed in the second
paragraph of his letter?

Editor's note: there are also—entirely by chance—a further two
US states to be found in the same paragraph that have joined the
Union since this letter was written to Poe in 1846.

BOARDERS' ENTERTAINMENT

I made the acquaintance of several boys during my brief time at boarding school in Chelsea, gaining a great insight into the formation of the different character types which I now observe time and again throughout my adult life.

There was one particular boy who had a great love for geography and would spend many an hour poring over an atlas which was his prized possession. He seemed unconcerned by the raucous games that would inevitably arise in the evenings, moving himself into an alcove where he would not be disturbed.

Being of a quiet disposition myself, I felt a certain kinship with the studious boy in the corner, and sometimes approached him to ask what he had discovered most recently in his reading.

I remember clearly one answer he gave, which struck me as more than usually cryptic:

"Edgar, I have learnt about that which has a mouth but will never speak; that which can be slender and gentle, or broad and tumultuous; and that which has a bed but never will sleep."

Of what did the boy speak?

BIBLICAL WRITINGS

Today I find myself distracted; beset with a multitude of images of unknown origin, in shades which I cannot recognize. I sit at my desk, feeling the familiar edges firm beneath my fingers, but can find no clarity of meaning in the words I read. The letters blur together, a jumble on a page of meaningless concoctions.

It gradually returns to me... the subject of the list I consider. I recall I was reflecting on the many pairs which can be found in the writings of the Old Testament; names which are inextricably tied to one another, as firm as a vow.

My tortured mind saw only this:

AEVDAEM

DAGOVLIAIDTH

SGOMODORORAMH

SADELMILSOAHN

As I continued to gaze upon this jumbled list in front of me, my mind finally quietened, and the words finally came into focus.

What biblical pairs did I read in this list?

THE SILENT BISHOP

L ong had I struggled across desolate land, my body aching with cold. I knew not how far I had come, for all sense of time and place had dissolved in the bitter air. The hazy shapes which rose and fell in the darkness around me were the only certainty, and what cruel uncertainty that certainty held.

At length, a tower loomed through the mist; a solid, imposing outline which did not shift. In such a world of mirages, I was drawn to it, and found it to be a church, simple in construction with a spire rising from a stone transept.

Some solace filtered into my soul, and I entered, glad of the shelter it provided from the freezing wind. I sank into a pew and gazed at the vaulted ceiling, sensing the spirits of congregations past still lingering among the beams.

As my eyes drifted back down to the place where I sat, I became aware of a message scratched on the wood of the pew in front. It read as follows:

Every mystery can be solved, and every truth can be found.
Search only here:
M M L J

I sat for some time, thinking on what the sequence of letters could mean.

Where specifically does the writer of the message believe every truth can be found?

FORTUNATO'S CARAFES

ortunato, the great wine expert, had drawn a measure of inky Rioja from a barrel in his cellar, and was swirling it around a bulbous glass, carefully separating in his mind the scents which were rising out of it. A rich aroma of

plum infiltrated his mind, recalling long days spent in the orchards of his youth. The more complex notes of leather and oak which followed awoke a familiar excitement in his heart, as it was these elusive tastes which caught his attention.

For the purpose of aerating his wines, Fortunato was in possession of two intricate cut-glass carafes, carefully engraved by the finest craftsmen. One of them held 5 pints, the other held 3 pints.

At length, he was visited by a fellow connoisseur, who had heard whispers of the great vintage in Fortunato's barrel, and wished to purchase some for himself.

"I will not deprive you of too much of the wine, Fortunato—I will be content with just one pint".

Fortunato's heart sank at this, for the carafes were his only measuring devices, and he did not wish to give a drop more than one pint to anyone with an inferior palate to himself. He held the glass up to the light of his candle and considered his predicament.

How could Fortunato measure out only one pint, without guessing or discarding any wine?

PROSPERO'S GUARDS

In the midst of the Red Death, the great plague that was sweeping the land under the rule of Prince Prospero, the ruler had banished all courtiers and servants from his chamber. The only two that remained were guards, solid of build, who he had retained to keep watch over the tower in which he slept.

Each morning, he instructed the guards to stand at the pinnacle of the tower, where they could look out across the battlements and observe the movements of the people who scuttled, antlike, at the foot of the walls. He instructed them each day to stand at opposite ends of the tower, one facing east and one facing west.

As he stood at the window one evening, watching the sun set over his troubled land, Prospero heard the guards outside talking together, one asking the other the reason for his fellow guard's troubled expression.

He fell into a state of contemplation. How could they see each other's faces while maintaining their stations facing east and west?

IN THE MONASTERY GARDEN

Prince Prospero had retreated once again to his abbey to hide from the many ills of the world. After he had partaken of a hearty meal, he took a stroll in the kitchen garden to observe the produce of the monks and to fill his lungs with clean air.

Sitting on a bench among the herbs and vegetables were two monks, both engrossed in a conversation about the manuscripts they had illuminated. Their words were cryptic, and the Prince lingered next to an aptly named sage bush to elucidate their meaning.

"Yesterday I embellished the corner of my page with a figure I find most beautiful. Such a figure can be found in both convent and nave, but never kitchen."

What had the monk drawn in his illumination?

39

THE
DARK NIGHT

I sat alone in my study one evening, poring over a volume of poetry which had lain disregarded at the back of a shelf for some time. The night was dark and, as I listened to the

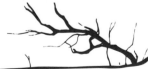

wind howling around the chimneys, the grim realization descended that my lamps were growing dim, and would soon be extinguished.

Not desiring to leave the confines of the room, I lit a candle and continued my perusal in its murky glow. My eyes grew weary in the gloom, and shapes began to swim around me, growing ever more twisted and nightmarish. The legs of a coat stand elongated and drew toward me with the steps of a terrible insect, the fireplace yawning its vast mouth as if to swallow me deep into its shadows.

From the corner of the room, something took my attention, tall and flickering in the dim light. Its eyeless face was pale, and it had no mouth with which to answer my startled cry. It stretched out ornate hands which had no fingers, and a cold sense of doom fell upon me as I listened to the rhythmic beating that betrayed its living heart.

As my eyes grew accustomed to the dark and the shapes began to clarify around me, I realized the true identity of this fearsome figure.

What was it?

THE TAILOR

I knew a man, many years ago, who cared greatly for fine apparel, and clothed himself with rich cuts of silk and velvet. Many a tailor had heard of his tastes, and they all made great effort with new patterns and fine materials to appeal to him.

It transpired after some years that the attention he gave to his wardrobe far exceeded the attention he paid to his wallet. The tailors thus tired of supplying him with silken hats and soft cravats, but rather than cut him off without a word, they devised a trick, by which he could be humiliated into repentance.

When he next visited the oldest and most highly regarded tailor, he was presented with a dilemma:

"My friend, your debts have grown impossible to ignore, but I put this to you—if you can answer my

question, I will charge you only half of
what you owe.

"I have here a pair of fine herringbone
trousers, made by my most skilled
seamstress. See the fine stitching on
the pockets!

"I challenge you to put them on,
and to insert your left hand into the
right pocket, and your right hand
into the left pocket, without crossing
your arms."

The man tried this and then failed.
He stood in a state of confusion, and
then sighed, for he could not devise
a method by which this could be
achieved.

The tailor knew that it was
possible—but how?

TWO INTO FIVE

In the natural lulls which occur while writing, I occasionally divert myself by considering the quirks of the English language, and particularly enjoy finding words that can be found concealed within others.

While flicking back through the pages of my notebook during a lonely hour, I found a list of such lexical puzzles. In each instance, there is one word which can be placed in between the two others, creating two further new words, one formed of the first and central words, and the other formed of the central and second words. In this way, each pair of two words becomes a group of five words once solved.

Here are three such pairs:

HERE _ _ _ _ _ WORD
OVER _ _ _ AWAY
BED _ _ _ _ MARK

Can you identify the missing word in each case?

A CHILL IN
THE AIR

I took a stroll one evening along the tree-lined avenues not far from my home. The air was crisp, heralding the return of shorter days and duller skies. I wrapped my coat closer about my frame and quickened my pace.

I began to consider the art of poetry, and how we synthesize the world in images. We cannot help but see the shapes of our childhood in the shadows thrown by racing clouds; equate the fluid glide of the heron with the movement of a dancer. A hive of bees will forever appear industrious to human eyes.

As I wandered, the familiar feeling descended upon me of words drifting, as if through water in my mind, ready to be assembled into sentences.

Born into balletic flight,
My patterned dress of purest white,
In life I settle; quiet. Still,
In death I run with giddy thrill.

What was the subject of my rhyme?

THE LONESOME BIRD

Before the dawn had stretched her listless limbs above the horizon, I had arisen from my bed to drift about my rooms, contemplating the various blues which precede the watery yellow of day.

I lingered at a window, meditating on the boughs of an ancient chestnut which stood outside, solid and gnarled with age. It was late in September, one of those mournful, golden days which herald the end of summer, and bring to mind the inevitability of beauty's dissolution into waste and cold. The birds could feel it, and let their song flow torpidly over the branches, thick as sap.

I have a familiarity with the birds from years of watching them through my window, and I recognize their calls. The finches, woodpeckers, and sparrows skim past each other, wings occasionally grazing each other in a flurry of feathers.

But one remains forever calm. Unmoving. He is a rook with beadlike eyes, perched on one of the highest branches, judging all with his stare.

He is a constant in the otherwise transient tangle of wood and leaves, and his countenance often inspires my mind. Indeed, just yesterday I wrote a poem about a rook that stood just as still, but it had not wings, eyes, or even feathers. What was the subject of my poem?

THE ATHLETE

One damp November evening, I was sat in one of my customary writing seats watching clouds gather over distant hills, shrouding the landscape in a dewy haze. As the light faded, my reverie was disturbed by a sudden movement on the road outside. Someone ran past, then into the distance and back into obscurity.

I thought nothing more of it until the following evening, when the same figure dashed past, at around the same time. My interest was aroused, and that evening I visited the local tavern where I sat at the bar to drink a glass of wine and observe proceedings.

The same gentleman who had progressed so swiftly past my window was sat in a corner. He was tall and lean, with an air of quiet focus. Next to him was a young man with an athletic build who was obviously mesmerized by the newcomer.

As I listened, the runner spoke of his adventures:

"I have run along desert tracks, across icy plains, and through the throng of cities. I have had many experiences and met people stranger than I could ever have imagined. But what perpetually enthrals me is that which can run for hundreds of miles, traverse landscapes of all kinds, and yet never move an inch."

What was he speaking of?

THE GRAVE–TENDER

There is a gentleman in Richmond of some advanced years, whose job it is to maintain the cemetery.

He rarely speaks, preferring the company of his tools, the undulating stems of the flowers which grow among the graves, and the boughs of birch which dapple the stones with purple and silver. I often pass him on my walks through the quiet paths, and our eyes sometimes meet with the unspoken affinity of mourners.

Once, when standing alone in the thickening heat of the afternoon, I overheard him speaking with what I took to be another visitor.

"Ah, here you are; the dearest friend I have ever known. What beautiful flowers you have brought today. And a new ring every year, yet never will you marry!".

This last he said with a laugh, as if the thought amused him.

Who was he talking to?

SHADOWY FIGURES

Shadows can have a remarkable effect on the most familiar of settings. Objects whose outlines are readily recognized when touched by the sun become twisted and sinister when darkness falls.

I find myself fascinated by this eerie metamorphosis, and often sit for many hours after night has fallen, meditating on my surroundings and observing the illusions which occur.

One such night I remember more clearly than others. My body was restless, my mind agitated with unresolved anxieties, and my gaze passed swiftly over the items which surrounded me, flickering between corners and spaces without rest.

I wandered further through my home, observing the contours of the rooms as they unfolded before my unfocused eyes. As I passed the sturdy wooden frame of a table, a line of eight figures caught my eye, stern-faced and military in stature, ready to move forward to protect their rulers.

What sight had captured my attention on my nocturnal walk?

THE STORMY RIDE

Riding out one morning without much idea as to where to steer my horse, I found myself following a route past a small icy lake. As I cast my gaze over its half-frozen top, memories began to float to the surface of my mind—memories of my visit to the fateful House of Usher some years past. I grappled with the swimming thoughts as I progressed along the lake's edge, for I knew the perils of sinking into the darkest corners of that terrible memory.

As I progressed, the sky began to darken and ripples carved deepening grooves on the unfrozen parts of the water. A grand house stood in the shadow of a hill some miles forward, and I resolved to take some shelter there while the storm ran its course.

On my arrival the courtyard was empty, but for two figures dressed in well-worn corduroy trousers who were replacing a broken tile on the roof of the stable block. Their faces were pale and, as they cast their eyes to the swirling skies, I saw the ghost of dismay pass across their brows.

I called out to them, asking if my horse could rest awhile in the stable, sheltered from the howling wind. They descended from their lofty perch, and I was suddenly taken aback at how alike the pair were, and asked if the two were brothers.

"He is my brother, but I am not his brother," came the cryptic reply from one of the pair, and the two dissolved in conspiratorial laughter.

How could this be the case?

THE PARTY

At one of the soirées of Ms. Birchwood, a gifted and imaginative artist, I was drawn into a conversation about various scandalous affairs and dubious business dealings that had been taking place in the state of New York over the previous months.

I remained at the periphery of the conversation and, as is often the way at such events, utterances began to crash into one another as the participants became more animated, propelled by the free-flowing cocktails that swirled in intricately decorated goblets.

"Mr. Redbridge has truly outdone himself. I heard that he has taken off to start a business with his father's nephew."

"His marriage as well, such a trauma for his wife—I heard that he filed for divorce in the middle of October and is living with a sculpture student in Albany."

"How extraordinary! I heard that he was eloping with his widow's sister to get married in Vermont."

"The whispers in Long Island are that he robbed his father's business partner's godson and took off with the cash on horseback."

I listened carefully to the conversation despite my silence, and frowned, for I had noticed that one person's claim was definitely false.

Which person was telling a lie?

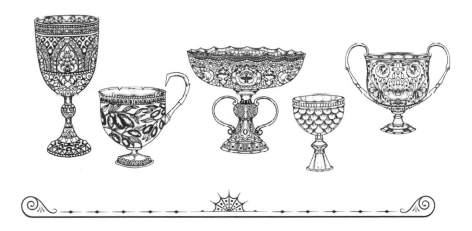

THE DARK ABODE

There was a woman who lived at the end of a narrow, undulating road in Richmond, riddled with holes and inhospitable to traverse. She never left her home, preferring to keep the company of the birds who roosted in her garden and a solitary black cat, which held not even a speck of white anywhere upon it.

I was often drawn down this avenue on my excursions. No lights illuminated her home at night, nor the road leading to it, and I found a comfort in the knowledge that I could pass untouched by the glare of lamps, and without witnessing the wild dance of a disturbed candle. Even the moon was lost behind the trees that towered above her residence.

On one occasion, while riding down this lane, I was forced to sharply tug on my horse's reins, stopping him so suddenly I nearly fell from my saddle. The black cat was stretched out on the ground, directly in my path, her eyes closed in a languorous sleep.

How was I able to see the cat in time to avoid trampling her?

THE PASSAGE OF TIME

What a mysterious thing the passage of time is. As a child, each day passes in a languid haze of warm grass and sweetness, with troubles drifting in and out, fleeting as clouds. But as adults, the cumuli move slower, lingering to dampen our days with cares.

Days and weeks blur. Tuesdays, Wednesdays, weekends, and holidays passing in an unfocused progression of dusks and dawns; the acceleration into the drudgery of advanced age looming on the horizon each new morning.

I once visited a physician who had invented a preparation which he claimed could reverse the effects of aging. He instructed me to place three drops beneath my tongue at midnight on the first day of each month with twenty-eight days, and to keep this strange ritual for a period of one year.

I raised my eyebrows, for there was something peculiar in his instruction.

"How many times do you anticipate I will take this preparation?", I questioned.

What was the answer to my question?

THE CAPTAIN'S PLIGHT

The branching rivers of the port of New York throng with ships, carrying cargoes that range from tea to passengers, immigrating to pursue their dreams in this land of hope and promise. Smoke rises in a haze over the docks as the steam ships navigate the windswept waters.

Sailors can often be found wandering the streets near the docks—and I remember clearly one conversation I overheard there:

"My ship docked in New York just this afternoon, stocked with a cargo of lumber from Canada. Over the past weeks I have been fashioning a ladder for our crew to climb to the upper decks more easily. It is made with strong rope and knotted firmly—yet I have a dilemma for you.

"The ladder is secured to the outside of the boat, and has eighteen rungs which stretch from the upper deck down to 3 feet above the water. Each rung is one foot apart. If the water was to rise at the rate of half a foot every hour, how long would it take before the ladder was completely submerged?"

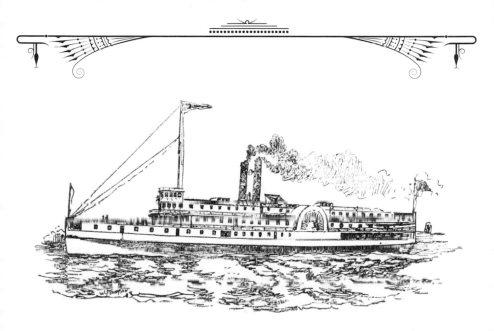

The other sailors laughed as I looked on, obviously unwilling to consider the solution.

What was the answer to the sailor's dilemma?

THE OLD
SCHOOLROOM

There is a house situated at the edge of a wood, in a quiet spot not often visited by the ramblers who frequent the more well-trodden paths. The marshy land which surrounds it has become overgrown with ferns since

it ceased to be inhabited some years ago, and the tendrils of climbing plants are beginning to make their steady advances up the panes of the windows.

It used to be an old schoolroom. Desks can still be seen through the window, and scraps of paper lie discarded and mouse-bitten upon the dusty floorboards.

I entered once in a moment of curiosity, wondering what exercises those discarded books contained. An old volume of mathematics lay on a desk at the front of the room, and in among the geometry and algebra was written a most perplexing question:

What number has its letters in alphabetical order when written as a word in English?

I took a seat at one of the dilapidated desks to muse upon this problem. I was there for some time, the light fading before I landed upon the correct answer.

What is the number?

A STRANGE ILLNESS

I am no stranger to the solitude of disease; to the hushed, withholding tones of doctors as they speak to the ill. The familiar sound of breath catching in the lungs—the harbinger of consumption—has haunted my ears all too often in my short life.

I try not to dwell on such things, and to keep the scourge of hypochondria at bay with thoughts of writing. But further, I try to bring a lightness of description to the inevitable conversations about health which arise during the course of daily life.

Just yesterday, when speaking with one of the New York newspaper editors with whom I have become acquainted, I languidly mentioned that I had a swiftly burgeoning growth on my head, which was causing me some concern.

He commented that this was not to be ignored, and that I should seek professional help, even recommending I visit a place he knew in Long Island.

I took his advice, but it was not to visit a doctor or other physician. Why not?

THE PROFESSOR'S PUZZLE

I vividly remember a certain visit to a university which used human cadavers in its medical lectures. The students would peer from the lofty benches, watching their professor make each incision, and gently tease apart the skin on either side of the cut to reveal the soft organs that lay beneath.

In conversation with one such professor on my visit, I asked him to relate some of the most memorable experiences of his career. He spoke at some length of the many universities he had visited, the students he had taught, and the hospitals at which he had advised. As he went on, my attention began to drift toward other matters, and was only brought back into the room by a strange statement from the man of medicine:

"I have seen bodies of all shapes, which have perished from all manner of maladies, but I maintain to this day that the most satisfying sight to my eyes has many hearts, and yet no lungs or stomach."

What was he talking about?

THE SHERRY CASKS

Fortunato had ordered five new casks of sherry for his collection, a fine Amontillado not easily accessible to those less knowledgeable about the more intricate qualities of wine.

He was not a humble man, and his enthusiastic discussions of this exceptional sherry had circulated among the various vineyard owners and wine enthusiasts of the area. Fortunato had resultantly found himself inundated with requests from people wanting to purchase an amount from his collection.

After sifting through the orders, he rejected all but three of the requests, which were from the wealthier and more distinguished of his acquaintances.

He decided to divide one full 7-gallon cask between them, giving two of the wine-lovers 2 gallons and then 3 gallons to the third man, the wealthiest of the three. However, he subsequently found that the only empty casks he had in his cellar would hold only 4 gallons and 3 gallons respectively.

How could Fortunato accurately divide the 7 gallons into two lots of 2 gallons and one lot of 3 gallons, using the 7-gallon, 4-gallon, and 3-gallon casks available? Assume he does not do so by eye, and does not use any other containers or tools.

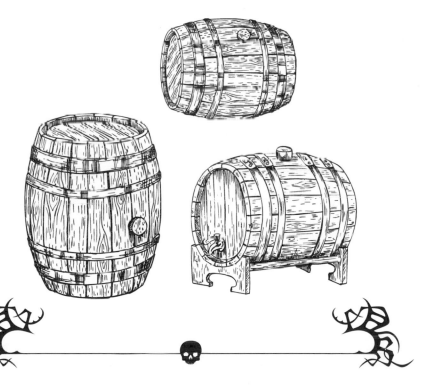

THE AVIARY

There is an aviary some miles from Boston, a strange place where iron cages rise from the ground, stern and draughty as churches. Their rafters are haunted by the calls of parakeets, and the nightingale greets each evening with a plaintive dirge.

It is run by a small, stooped man who wanders the passages between his avian charges in a long black coat, dispensing food from a canister kept about his neck. He counts the birds daily, giving no care to their flitting movements. He knows them all, their habits and mannerisms, and has no interest in the troubles of man.

He is known for being particular about numbers, and it is said that he keeps exactly 1,500 birds at all times in total across the three cages, each of different size, with one cage containing precisely four times the number of another, and one cage containing precisely ten times the number of another.

How many birds are in each of the three cages?

FROM THE EDITOR 2

The latest submission I received from the editor of the *Messenger* came with a note, written in an unsettlingly neat hand which sloped slightly to the left, as if it had been blown across the page by a strong wind.

Dear Mr. Poe,

I was most intrigued to read your request for coded text. I have long had an interest in the different methods through which messages can be concealed, for purposes both virtuous and nefarious. My interests, however, are purely recreational, and I challenge you to decode the sunny place of my birth:

T_E _R_N_H _I_R_

Yours sincerely,
Mr. J. Lovell Esq.

Where was Mr. Lovell born?

THE BLESSING

I find the silence which comes with the winter months to be a great solace after the raucous cacophony of summer. I often look to the sky, eager for the sight of the first migrating flocks, their formation tracing triumphant lines of seasonal division across the clouds.

I was walking through the streets of Richmond on one such cool, quiet evening, tasting the tang of impending frost on the chill air, when I chanced to meet upon a gentleman familiar to many in the town.

As our paths crossed, he greeted me with a tip of his hat, which I returned in a gesture of silent respect.

On the far side of the road, I became aware of another familiar face, a woman pruning the trees which arched over her garden gate. The gentleman called in greeting to her in his penetrating, sonorous voice, and then moved on. I lingered in thought for a moment and, as I hesitated, the woman spoke to me:

"Such a kind man, that one—yet I pity him. I cannot imagine what it must be like to be him. Father to so many, and yet never any children."

How is this possible?

THE BATHROOM

I do not often dwell on my own reflection. I find the contours of my face are most at home in the restless glow of candlelight, disordered by shadows; not illuminated for the scrutiny of those other eyes which might wish to seek out beauty.

Despite this tendency to visual obscurity, I find the maintenance of a small moustache to be of benefit to the ensemble of my features, and keep a shaving set to hand by the basin with which to groom it periodically.

Sometimes, while in the throes of the shaving ritual, I think on the time expended on editing our faces thus, reinventing our visage while cropping what is left of our lives. I sometimes in turn consider others I know with complex facial hair.

Indeed, I know a man who shaves each and every day without fail, but without his hair ever getting any shorter.

How can this be?

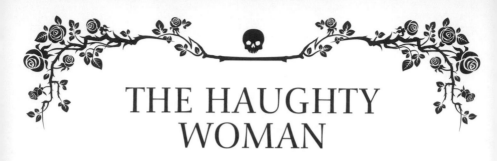

THE HAUGHTY
WOMAN

There is a woman I once knew in Richmond, a tall lady with a gaunt face, who looked at the world as if all she gazed upon fell short of expectation. It was nigh impossible to strike up conversation with her, and she was mostly seen

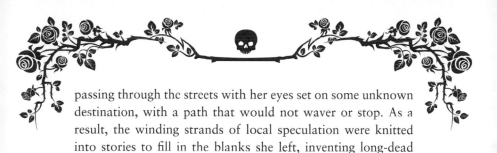

passing through the streets with her eyes set on some unknown destination, with a path that would not waver or stop. As a result, the winding strands of local speculation were knitted into stories to fill in the blanks she left, inventing long-dead husbands, sisters shunned by society, and all manner of estranged children.

I would listen intently to such anecdotes, and gained a respect for the lady as I realized that she fed her critics with carefully formulated stories, designed to confound and even menace. One afternoon, I heard a young butcher's apprentice say to his friend:

"I heard her just yesterday say, 'I have captured the man I love—his head lies perfectly still, caged behind the door of a chamber. Here he shall stay until I die, his memory heavy on my chest.' I reckon she's murdered someone!"

I smirked to myself and turned away from his ludicrous remark—for I knew that the lady referred to something much more material than murder.

What did the lady's riddle refer to?

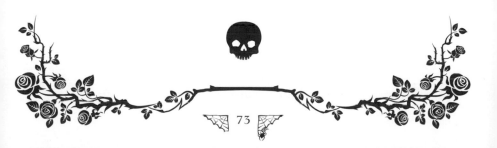

TWO INTO FIVE AGAIN

In the search for inspiration for a new story, I found myself revisiting old notes in the hope of finding some previously overlooked description. Alas, my search yielded little, although I did find a selection of further word puzzles, written in so shaky a hand I must have written under the influence of some moonlit distortion.

For each line below, there is one word which can fit between the two others, creating two further new words, one formed of the first and central words, and the other formed of the central and second words. In this way, each pair of two words becomes a group of five words once solved.

KNEE _ _ _ ABLE
HARD _ _ _ _ MATE
ANY _ _ _ LAYS

Which three words were missing?

NIGHTMARE IN THE STORM

Though the descent into tormented sleep is so often one of distress and desolation, I find a certain fascination in the visions which arise when deep sleep has set in.

Last night, in the midst of a tumultuous storm, I dreamed

of a strange spirit, who came to me in my own room, drifting between the curtains and darting over the books which are piled in shadowy corners.

"Who are you, spirit?", I asked, dreading an omen of my impending doom.

"I am the child of those who race through the sky, the constant shape-shifters who dance with the wind. I give birth to the currents of the river, and when I come to rest I give life to everything I find."

What did the spirit that came to me embody?

THE APOTHECARY

In the middle of Baltimore there is an old apothecary with a wooden front and a window facing out onto the street, filled with dusty bottles of tinctures to aid ailments of every kind. If you look closely, you can see the leeches writhing over each other, waiting for their next sanguineous meal.

It is run by a small woman with yellowing white hair, which hangs, listless and lifeless, about her shoulders, and darting eyes which keenly observe the every move of those who enter.

Last week I visited her establishment to collect a preparation of laudanum, for my sleep had been much disturbed. As I entered, I saw her standing at the counter, contemplating an empty medicine jar of no small size. It seemed that a single black feather had somehow drifted and landed inside the bottle. This cursed symbol needed immediate vanquishing.

The bottle neck was too thin for her to reach in and grasp the unwanted object. I asked her why she could not simply tip it out, and she explained that it was a display item that was firmly secured to the surface of the counter. She then tried blowing into the bottle, but the feather was not keen to exit, and her attempt to fetch it out with string or wire also failed.

How else could the feather be easily removed without moving the bottle?

FROM THE EDITOR 3

In this week's set of submissions from the *Messenger*, I received another letter from the gentleman who had written to me some months previously of his tour of the states of America. This time, it appeared that he had visited France. Or at least his letter claimed as much.

> *Dear Mr. Poe,*
>
> *I write to you once again of my travels, this time to inform you that, since I fell ill, even I have taken up aristocratic tendencies in my old age. I now find it very nice to ride a fine white mare along the tracks of the French countryside, past the indignant estates of meagre nobles. The paths of the forest are musical aisles of birdsong, the thrushes singing sweetly on the boughs. I am reminded of the American nesting birds, although they lack their variety.*
>
> *I wonder if you can find my next collection of destinations...*
>
> *Yours truly,*
> *Mr. A D Camore*

Mr. Camore had concealed eight well-known French towns and cities in the text of his letter. What are the names of those towns and cities?

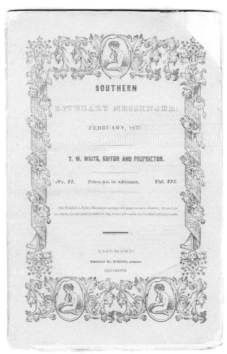

A LETTER FROM FANNY

I received a letter from Mrs. Sargent Osgood this week, a particularly talented writer whom I have had the pleasure of getting to know through Nathaniel Parker Willis. She is a true Sirius in the constellation of writers which moves across our sky, her words sitting most luminously upon the page.

This week she wrote to me with a curious dilemma:

Dear Mr. Poe,

I am hearing constantly of advances in science and mathematics; enchanting formulas to explain the mysteries of our universe. Yet I myself, a woman without advanced mathematical education, have managed to come up with a formula which defies the logic of such systems…

How can I take four away from seven and be left with five? And in the exact same way, how can I take two away from five and be left with four?

I hope my little problem will entertain you as the days grow shorter and the cold months encroach once again upon our comfort.

Yours truly,
Fanny

How could Mrs. Osgood's observations be explained?

THE NIGHTMARE

Each night that I am spared the swirling visions of unquiet dreams is such sweet release; a peaceful expanse of water to carry my soul undisturbed through those hours that remain stubbornly lacking in sunlight.

But this never lasts. I am too familiar with the tumultuous tendencies of my mind and know that, even while swimming in this tranquil lake of dreams, the skies may darken and those many-winged spirits of hell will descend to drag me into the degraded depths of my own subconscious.

Last night, I dreamed of a spirit with fire in her eyes. Her form was that of my own sister, and it was all I could do not to call her name. She was clothed in white lace, but dull stains of blood crept over her cuff like the dreaded gait of a spider.

She spoke to me in my sister's voice, hemmed with spectral fury:

> "For all of your knowledge of science, and enthusiasm for reasoning, you always carry the same question about these dreams. You hang on to the fervent hope that its answer is 'yes', and dread it may ever be 'no'. And yet you may never truthfully answer 'yes' while you are conscious."

What was the question the ghostly figure spoke of?

THE END OF THE LESSON

Writing is a slow and arduous process! Thoughts circulate around my mind like starlings, flocking together for brief seconds before dispersing in a spinning murmuration.

I chanced to walk past the town schoolroom on one of my recent outings to clear my head. It was a dark afternoon on one of those February days where the light never seems to fully penetrate through the clouds, and the world is illuminated only by a faint ashen glow. I was drawn, moth-like, to the glow of the classroom window and, as I peered through, I saw the schoolmaster erasing the previous lesson from the board. Yet he was called away from his task by a voice from elsewhere, and a collection of letters were left running in a column down the left-hand side of the board. They had each been the initial letter of a sequence of words:

T
T
F
F
S
S

I was intrigued to know the subject of the lesson, and committed the sequence to memory. As I walked further, I found my thoughts crystallizing, and the answer gradually flowing into my mind.

What would be the next letter in the sequence, and why?

THE GUARD DOG

There is a man who lives alone in a secluded house on the outskirts of Richmond, far from the hubbub of the downtown areas. He seldom goes out but, when he does, he speaks to no one in any social way, confining his interactions to a few short words with shopkeepers.

He is in possession of a notoriously large dog, a towering beast with jet-black fur. The people in the town learned long ago not to cross him and so give the house a wide berth, but from time to time a foreign visitor will rouse the hound and trigger a volley of loud barks.

On one occasion I myself was just such a foreign visitor. I passed by his house but, being soft of foot, managed to pass by without waking the sleeping beast and invoking his wrath. I did observe, however, that the dog was securely tied to a rope of around 10 feet in length, and lying in the shade of a large elm tree.

I stopped a little way off to observe my surroundings and, as I stood anonymous under a friendly oak some distance away, I noticed the animal stretch his limbs and wake, then walk toward a water trough from which he took a deep drink. By a rough estimate, however, it was around 40 feet from the hound's familiar position.

How would it have been possible for the dog to drink from the trough while tied to the 10-foot rope?

A QUIET MOMENT

How the torrent of life streams around us, in its unending cascade of cares. There is no escaping the current, and as the darkness of evening draws in around me I all too often sense that I am being borne forward in a direction I do not wish to travel, unprotected by the blind seraphs of hope.

My age is the current cause of my distress. My brother was two years older, while he lived, and my father had me at 25. Although my father passed away long ago, and consumption sent my brother to an early grave, it has come to me, in the sudden manner of a rainstorm in July, that were they both still living then our combined ages as of this day would be 135.

So how old am I?

THE MOURNERS

A h, the solemn expressions of mourners, and the silver crescents of their faces. They cast such an ethereal pall, draped in their black veils, shining with lunary beauty. In such stately repose is that celebration of death, washing the deceased clean with melancholy dirges and cryptic rites

I once discussed such rites with a well-known mathematician. He had planned his funeral extensively, and related to me his formula.

Seventy mourners were to attend his body in total while he lay in his family crypt for a period of exactly four days. Each day, five more mourners would visit than had done so on the previous day.

"What a challenge it will be for them", he declared with twisted glee. "Just yesterday I asked my son how many mourners would visit me on the third day, and he could not answer me."

How many mourners would be scheduled to visit the mathematician's body on the third day?

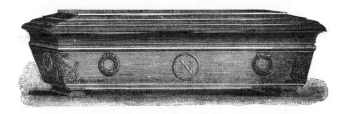

THE SPECTRAL SEA

One evening, I took a stroll through Richmond to clear my head, basking in the hazy dusk that weaved in and out of the rooftops.

On my way, I passed a small cottage which I have often observed with intrigue. Its windowsills are invariably layered with dust, and the peeling paint on the front door gives the entrance a menacing air. This day, I observed the door to be open.

Unable to control my curiosity, I entered. It was plainly the house of a sailor, being filled with books on knots and the various types of communication used at sea.

I had not been in the hallway more than a minute when a large grandfather clock rang out, announcing the time as half past midnight. The house held an eerie draw for me, so I paused to ponder the mystery of the open door, wondering if the seafarer would soon return home. As I stood, I heard the clock sound a further six times, at a quarter to three, a quarter to eleven, a quarter past one, twenty past eight, ten past six, and once again at half past midnight.

A sense of understanding suddenly came over me: I knew the sailor was dead, and I, to my regret, knew the manner of his passing. So now I put the question to you—how did he die?

THE FLIGHT OF FANCY

I present to you a poem that came into my possession.
I shall not say how:

> A wraith-like figure came into sight,
> Clothed from head to toe in white,
> And all alone while rain did moan,
> This spectre spoke to me:

"After the swallow has long departed,
And post the heron has cleared the pond,
Once the egret has been outsmarted,
Still my heart will ache.

"Once the cormorant has built her nest,
The hawk has hunted and fed her young,
The owl has found a place to rest,
Still I will not wake.

"After the kestrel has dived and wheeled,
The eagle disembowelled her prey,
After the dove has passed the field,
Still my soul will break.

"Now I drift among the birds,
My death sung in their glossy notes.
Put my demise now into words,
In the hope my murderer recants."

I now ask you this: how did the wraith die?

THE CAT

I have always had such respect and admiration for the economical elegance of a cat's jump. True, the creatures themselves exist with a bad-natured disdain for humans, certain in their knowledge that they themselves know more of the universe than any human could ever hope to do.

There is one such arrogant creature that dwells not so far from my own residence, with a foolhardy approach to hunting. I see him often, leaping from high walls or balancing on precarious boughs in futile attempts to pluck a bird from a nearby branch.

Then just last week I observed him staring down at his prey from a nearby window ledge. I could not see the quarry he chased, but my heart twisted for the ledge was on the tallest tower of the building. For all of his nine lives, there was no recovery possible from a fall out of that window. But presently, he jumped —and yet I later saw he remained completely unharmed.

How could this have been?

THE GARDEN OF DEATH

The churchyard in Richmond holds many ancient and ornate graves, and I take a great interest in wandering among them, reading aloud the names and considering what little I learn of the lives of the dead from their brief epitaphs.

One afternoon, during one such wandering, I came upon a young man concealed within a cowl of fine drizzle, his face haggard with both rain and misery. I offered the man a sip from my flask to warm his body and soothe his soul, whereupon he spoke to me in a voice wracked with a bleak and solitary sadness that I will not soon forget:

"Just yesterday, I married the woman I love."

Such happy words, when written plain, and yet not for him the joys of the matrimonial contract. I wondered then how many of the gravestones' writings concealed a lifetime of misery in their flowery phrases of cadaverous repose.

We sat a while in silence, observing the gravestones washing themselves clean in truly diluvial fashion.

Why was the man so forlorn?

THE MENAGERIE OF DOOM

In the darkness of my dreams last night, a foul mass of creatures descended upon me. I knew not where I was, and no buildings were in sight to navigate by, only the twisted boughs of windswept trees.

Without warning I was beset by a whirlwind of beetles, their great green abdomens thrumming with the gravity of their rage. They swept over me, a terrible winged army. They passed swiftly, but as they circled around to plague me once more, I saw that in their wake ran a monstrous cluster of spiders, and soon felt the frantic scrambling of their legs across my flesh.

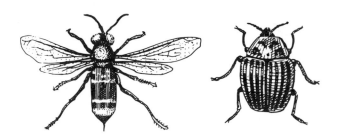

I searched around, desperately seeking for something to distract the terrible creatures. My fingers closed around an apple, and I gathered enough strength to roll it toward the oncoming beasts. Some were distracted by the fruit, and diverted their path toward it. As the awful tide parted, I became transfixed by the movement of their legs.

In my grim trance I began to count the creatures that advanced toward the apple. Their 19 heads and 134 legs moved steadily forwards with fitful, alien movements.

How many beetles and spiders had I counted, taking into account that the spiders in my dream had eight legs and the beetles had six?

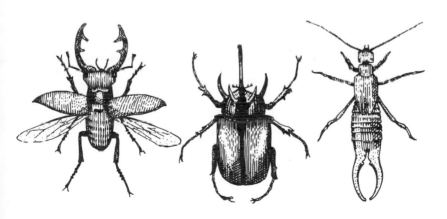

A CONCERTO OF MYSTERY

This week's delivery from the *Messenger* concerned an issue which had been troubling musicians in the area for several weeks. Various pieces of musical paraphernalia had been going missing: bows, rosin, strings, footstools, and such like. The police had narrowed down the suspects to the members of a local chamber orchestra, but had no further leads on who exactly the culprit might be.

> *Mr. Poe,*
> *I know who is guilty of these crimes—but I leave it to your cryptographic skills to solve the final steps of the mystery:*
>
> IT HB CE
> LJ DE AA DB
> LV HI OM GL AA
> PF EL AA SY CE RP
> DI SR
> CG SU ID IL JT YW
>
> *Your sincere friend,*
> *A Music Lover*

Who was the thief?

A LETTER FROM OSGOOD

I was both pleased and surprised to once again receive a letter from Mrs. Sargent Osgood yesterday.

She knows, of course, of my enthusiasm for codes and ciphers. She must have taken this to heart, for along with a most entertaining letter detailing the trifling concerns of daily life (the contents of which I will not disclose), she included a mysterious message:

Emteemotomrrwotaudks.

It was a small matter to decipher the lady's message—but it made me wonder what else she might have to say...

What did the message read?

THE EXTENDED FAMILY

There is a large, rambling mansion on the outskirts of Richmond, the estate of a family who had made their millions farming cattle in the south. Their parties were legendary for the superior wine and lavish buffets offered, and invitations were highly sought after.

I recently attended a soirée at which I met a distinguished lady who had been the lucky recipient of one such sought-after invitation and she detailed to me the various intriguing attendees she had spoken to.

The family sounded an eclectic mix. The grandmother, a shrewd businesswoman who had quietly manipulated her husband and sons to build their empire, was due to turn 94. The youngest son, who had taken charge of the financial running of the company, had attended with his heavily pregnant wife, a woman of 27 clothed in a dark shade of maroon. The eldest son, a brash fellow of 43 who seldom spoke in praise of anyone, had attended alone and consumed a quite astonishing quantity of brandy.

"Quite a miscellany," declared a gentleman prone to mischievous utterances, "but do tell, who was the youngest there?"

A smile flitted, transient as a cloud, across my face.

Who was likely to have been the youngest at the party?

BEASTS OF MYTH

I have long been intrigued by the silver-tongued Sphinx, catching unsuspecting wanderers in her net of riddles; the sweeping wings of the Roc; and the dreaded scales of the Cockatrice. The names of such legendary beasts have a resonance to them, a certain tang when held under the tongue.

Flicking through the pages of my notebook, I often find mysterious lists—perhaps ideas for narratives, descriptions of accursed settings, or the names of the villains that haunt them. I recently found one such list, in which I had concealed the names of three mythical creatures, one in each sentence.

As I renounce my claim, I shall let the house fade into moonlight.
I see it glow, bathed in the light of its pearlescent aura.
I must complete this grim antic, or else I shall lose her love forever.

What were the names of the creatures I had concealed?

THE BLACK CAT

There is a quiet, secretive gentleman who lives in a diminutive cottage on my street. I have never known his name, nor indeed much at all save that he is the custodian of a large black cat; a most splendid creature with a lustrous fur that glows with a blue tint as the moon sails her ghostly course through the clouds. I often observe him as he stalks, near-invisible, through the winding passages of the town.

How I envy the solitude of this beast; his freedom to bask in the glow of night unhindered by the sundry affairs which trouble his human companions. At times I consider possessing such an animal—not that such independent dignity would ever consider itself possessed.

Yet, my mind returns, inevitably to that which I do possess: a companion which comes and goes with the passage of the days, yet who vanishes for hours on end—but whom I will never lose.

Who is this companion?

A VISIT FROM MRS. SARGENT OSGOOD

My communications with Mrs. Sargent Osgood have taken an interesting turn of late, and I often feel a certain apprehension about her visits.

On one of her recent visits, during a particularly bold exchange, I took the liberty of asking her age. A piercing look in my direction felt intended to quell my inquiry, and yet Mrs. Osgood answered my question, albeit in somewhat cryptic terms.

"When today returns but six years hence, I shall be three times the age I was full eighteen years before today."

How old is she today?

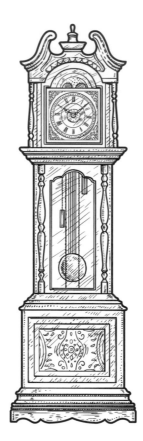

A TIMELY PURCHASE

I find the presence of clocks to be vital in any home—the regular ticking of their hands grounding one in the inescapable nature of mortality.

There came a point last year, however, when an ancient clock of mine fell to an unfortunate but rather permanent demise, and I found myself in need of the services of a clockmaker. I knew of a well-regarded man of this profession by the name of Arundel, and visited his workshop in order to choose a new timepiece.

I found two clocks which would suit my purpose, a carriage clock and a grandfather clock. The young assistant in the shop informed me that the carriage clocks could lose up to one minute every day. The grandfather clocks, on the other hand, were accurate to the nearest second on their first day but then, as their pendulum slowed, this possible loss of time would double each day.

If I were to set both clocks running, and each was to lose the maximum amount of time each day, how many days would it be before the grandfather clock could be more incorrect than the carriage clock?

FLOWERS FOR THE DEAD

My most recent journey through the graveyard yielded a sight as beautiful as it was harrowing. A new stone had been lain, its engraving still bright and fresh. Around it lay a profusion of white flowers, softly spreading their scent through the darkening air. Some were fresh, while others lay wilted or dead from days left in the sun.

I lingered awhile and, as I stood, partially concealed behind an ancient yew, I witnessed an elderly woman in expensive clothes approach the carpet of blooms. In her left hand she carried a basket, from which she drew some delicate white flowers.

I approached the lady and gave her my condolences for her loss. Her eyes were glazed as she replied.

"The first day I came, I brought one bloom. The day after that, I brought two, and I have brought one more bloom each day than I brought the day before. I will only cease when there are more than one hundred—one for each year that they lived."

How many days would the woman attend before 100 flowers lay on the grave?

AN EVENING OUT

I was readying myself to venture out for the evening. My destination was a soirée at the house of one of the more accommodating hostesses I had made the acquaintance of through my contact with the *Southern Literary Messenger*. She was known for her remarkable attention to detail with regard to fashion, and I vowed to make more effort than usual in clothing myself for the occasion.

The light faded fast as the evening descended on the process of my dressing, and I soon found myself plunged into darkness. On searching for candles, the dispiriting realization struck me that I had none left anywhere on the premises.

Luckily I had just my cufflinks left to put on. I also happened to know that in a certain drawer, due to repeated gifts, I had four cufflinks in the shape of magpies, four shaped like swallows, and four with the form of ravens.

How many cufflinks would I have to take out of the drawer in order to be certain of holding two with the same bird upon them?

A VISITOR FROM THE SOUTH

I occasionally entertain myself by casting my eyes over the writings of newspapers published in the diverse regions of this expansive and beguiling country. There are many stories from small towns of the south, detailing local issues which, though no doubt pressing to the inhabitants of the locale, seem alien to a writer who lives among the tumult of the city.

I read a story recently of a most unwelcome visitor to one such town, who in her swift visit had caused a great deal of distress. She had vandalized properties, ripped plants from gardens, broken windows, and thrown property into the air. In short, she had caused a great deal of damage and upset. Yet the legal system of the town had no interest in her, and she left the town unpenalized.

Who was this mysterious visitor?

THE SIGN IN THE BREEZE

I rode out early one morning, before the sun had fully flooded the world with its harsh illumination, nudging my horse into a trot across the wintry landscape that stretched out before me.

I chose a route which I had not yet traversed, intending to refresh my troubled mind with new sights. After an hour or so of riding through misty fields, I arrived at a hotel, a ramshackle building with a sagging doorframe and a rusty sign that proclaimed "VACANCIES". The roof was throbbing with starlings, and in a poor state of repair.

I noticed some letters etched into a plank of wood near the front door, and drew my mount closer to read what it conveyed. I was about to dismiss the garbled letters as the work of a mindless vandal, but something about the composition of the letters retained my attention:

STRUN
GAR, ANTA
R UT YIO
R PAREL

After studying the strange sight for a few minutes, I turned my horse sharply, and cantered back the way I had come.

What did the sign read which had caused me to retreat so hastily?

THE FAMILY
HISTORIAN

A letter arrived from the *Messenger*:

Dear Mr. Poe,
My attention was caught by your advertisement in the newspaper, not because I have a great desire to try to outwit you, as I'm sure many do, but because I have a problem which I thought you might perchance be able to help with.

I recently took possession of various family records, detailing the states in which five of my relatives worked. Unfortunately, the record is old, and various folds and stains along with the natural fading of ink over time have left the list of states fragmented, with many letters missing.

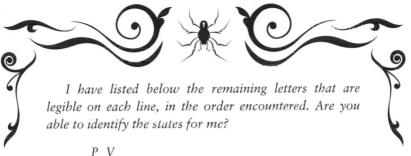

I have listed below the remaining letters that are legible on each line, in the order encountered. Are you able to identify the states for me?

P V
I S P
C K
J
E P

Yours,
Reginald G. Cuthbertson

To my mind the problem was trivial and I was pleased to be able to write back to the editor almost immediately.

What were the names of the five US states?

THE WRITER'S WAGES

A las, the most reliable form of income for writers at this moment in history is the critical review. The more scathing the comments, and the greater the dismemberment of the author, the more likely it is to be well-received—and the more its writer is likely to rise in the estimation of their editors.

Newspapers are peculiar institutions, and offer wages in forms which seem designed to confuse and bamboozle the average scribe, generally not known for their mathematical agility. Two newspapers recently offered me two different systems of payment in return for my writing.

The *Messenger* wrote informing me that I should receive $24 per month for my contributions, rising by one dollar each month I stayed with them. The *Post*, by contrast, offered an annual salary of $350 dollars.

Which newspaper offered the better remuneration for my writing, assuming I worked for exactly one year?

A FURTHER LETTER FROM FANNY

Having been in receipt of a poem of my own devising in which I had concealed her name, Mrs. Sargent Osgood wrote back to me with a puzzle of her own. She had composed a verse with seven missing words, which all shared a similar property. The missing word in each line of the poem was comprised of the same letters in the same order as the missing word in the previous line, but with one letter removed. It read as follows:

A noble lady, tall of _____, her plaintive calling all in vain,
She ceases walking, ceases talking, still as a _____ in the rain.
Her _____ of being, way of seeing, changed forever in just one day.
_____ her hunger with joy and care; send a sign to guide her way.
To the window where she _____ and watched the seasons change, evolve,
_____ peace with life and all its quirks, no strife to manage, riddle to solve.
_____ simple landscape of blossom and boughs, shading a world devoid of pain.

What words were missing from her poem?

AN ELEMENTAL ONSLAUGHT

I have sensed the coming storm for some days now. There is a certain charged stillness in the air; a change in the way the birds loop past the glowering eyes of the knots on the tree trunks. I cannot help but gain a small thrill from this lull, and relish the animal feeling of foreboding which grows in my chest as the sky grows dark.

When the rain begins, I will be well-prepared. My larder is stocked, my inkpot full, and I am content to confine myself for as long as it takes; until the clouds have visited the full extent of their rage upon the fields and houses that surround me.

Sudden streaks of lightning illuminate the still-darkening skies, harbingers of thunder's maniacal drumming. Several such storms have occurred during my life, and I know that it will be mere hours before rivulets form in the road that snakes past my window, sweeping the detritus in their path along their tumultuous journey.

As I gaze out of the window, watching the skirts of the cumulonimbi sweep across the horizon, I ponder upon the dampening trees, the destruction and regeneration that comes with each passing storm. It strikes me that there is something on this earth, well-known to all, that does not suffer from such torrents, and becomes no wetter in a storm, however hard the deluge.

What was I thinking of?

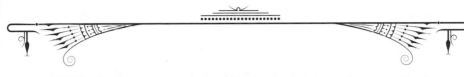

THE SOLITARY
FARMHAND

In the vast expanse of the American landscape, it is not difficult to travel outside of the hustle of city life; to transport oneself to the rural environs of the countryside, where the primary concerns are far from the luxury goods

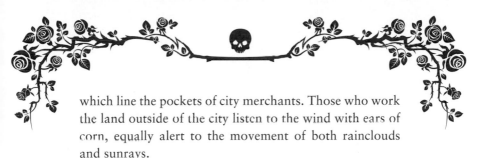

which line the pockets of city merchants. Those who work the land outside of the city listen to the wind with ears of corn, equally alert to the movement of both rainclouds and sunrays.

It came about one September that I had to make a long journey, which took me past several racing stud farms. When stopping to rest awhile, I chanced to speak to a young farmhand at one such establishment who had just finished oiling a collection of bridles and was beginning to clean out a stable block.

After some questioning, he told me that it took him four hours to clean out each block to his satisfaction, and that each block housed 26 animals. There were 7 blocks on the farmstead, each with 10 water buckets. Each water bucket served two animals.

After he had finished cleaning three blocks, how many cows were drinking out of clean buckets?

THE CANDLEMAKER'S CONUNDRUM

Here is an old story of a candlemaker who lived in the shadowy streets of downtown Boston, dealing his wares to those bold enough to venture through the throngs of pickpockets and street hawkers and into the quiet gloom of his establishment. I walked out one evening to visit him, as my stock of tapers for nighttime writing was much depleted.

The shopkeeper and myself were the only two in the store on this occasion, and the high shelves and low light gave a curious impression of the walls leaning in toward us. "Light is a many-fingered lady," he said as he reached up between the jars of tallow; "a magician with many tricks up her sleeve."

He lit a candle with an expert flick of a match.

"See, even now, as I light this candle, the size of four things in this very room changes. And yet as I light a second candle, their size decreases once again."

What was it that had decreased? It was not the shadows that he referred to.

THE WOMAN IN WHITE

As I passed the curling iron gate of the graveyard, I became aware of a figure standing near the central point of the plot, where the stones are the oldest. She was clothed in a white dress of a light material, and the wind curled around her in the hazy morning light, giving a luminous, spectral effect.

Our paths crossed as I walked on through, and as I stopped to let her pass she spoke to me in a thin voice cut through with the familiar rasp of illness.

"How strange it is, to see one's own resting place; the grass and flowers which one's own corpse will feed." A pause, and "I come here each morning to comfort the ghosts which rest in the soil; my relatives whom I will soon join."

She then described a strange, ineffable thing: "Look closely, here—can you see it in front of you? It is close to you and constantly moving; obscure to you—and yet you may alter it if you wish."

I remained still, unable to move under the weight of her words and the sadness they brought to my mortal frame.

What was this strange thing that the woman spoke of?

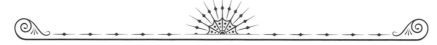

THE CELLAR AND THE COIN

One uncommonly fine September afternoon, my spirits were roused by the golden light dappling through the trees and so I decided to take a walk.

After an hour or so of contemplative perambulation, I found that my passage had wended its way through one of the vineyards of Baltimore to a wine cellar which I often frequented.

I came across the proprietor in the solace of the cool vaults, who drew me a glass of Médoc, passed me an apparently empty bottle, and spoke to me in bewildered tones.

"My friend, yesterday a fellow vintner brought me this firmly corked bottle into which he had placed a coin before then sealing it with the cork. He then challenged me to extract the coin without removing the cork, or causing any damage to the bottle."

The green glint of the bottle seemed to mock me, but I eventually thought of a solution.

How did I remove the coin?

THE BOOKSELLER'S CODE

There is a bookseller on the corner of two New York streets that I often traversed during my time in the city, an establishment with an old, once-green door and a creaking sign. Its interior is a winding warren of shelves and corridors, some passages blocked by the piles of books which have accumulated in them.

When passing one morning, I noticed that a sign had appeared in the window, detailing the prices of different genres.

Academic courses – 6¢
Classics – 4¢
Encyclopedias – 4¢
Romance – 2¢
Sheet Music – 2¢

I realized that there was a simple system that had been used to price this list, and quietly applauded the bookseller on his hidden code.

By what simple, consistent method had the books been priced?

THE IMPUDENT
CRITIC

A letter arrived from the *Messenger* this morning which I found most trying to my patience. The writer obviously thought himself to be a man of sagacity and wit, for he had the nerve to send a list that was close to my own heart.

Dear Mr. Poe,
I have become acquainted with the fact that you are a keen cryptographer, searching for problems to solve. I have compiled a list, somewhat literary in nature one might say, for you to cast your eye over. I trust it provides some entertainment.

Arono ele
Odalli tnomafo k saceht
Htaed derehtf oeuq sameht
Eugromeureht nisre drumeht

Yours sincerely,
An Avid Reader

What four literary entries are encoded in this list?

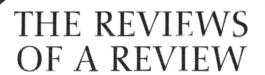

THE REVIEWS
OF A REVIEW

From time to time I write reviews for the *Southern Literary Messenger*, and the response to my latest critique has been particularly voluminous. My comments seem to have sparked an emotional reaction from many of the readers.

On Monday, I received a stack of letters, each addressed to me. On each of the subsequent days through until Friday, a total of four more letters than the number received on the preceding day were delivered. By Friday I therefore had 70 letters on my desk. How many letters had I had on Thursday in total?

A GRAVE CONCERN

There is a story in Richmond, whispered on misty evenings, of a woman who once lived confined within the walls of her rooms, leaving only once each year at midnight on All Souls Day to walk the streets in pensive silence.

Some claimed that her name had been Esther, and that after the death of her sister she was so consumed by grief that she had vowed never to leave the house in which they lived together, keeping their possessions ordered exactly as they were at the time of her sister's passing.

After some years of hearing this story reverberate in the quiet corners of conversation, I became consumed by intrigue, and took myself to the cemetery in search of her grave.

I found it soon enough, though her name was hard to make out beneath the moss and weeds that grew around the crumbling stone.

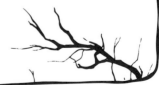

A faint inscription lay beneath the sisters' names, but age and lack of care had worn away alternate letters from the stone:

T_G_T_E_,   I_ L_F_ A_D _E_T_

After standing by the forgotten patch of soil for some time, I took my leave, sighing at the epitaph.

What had it once read?

THE FUNERAL

It was a Saturday in which the sun seemed never to fully venture above the horizon, leaving the rough grass of the cemetery bathed in a cheerless wash of half-light.

I was walking among the tombs and stone seraphs, on the way to the resting place of my darling Virginia. Three white roses were in my hands, and I touched one momentarily to my cheek to recall the softness of her face on mine.

As I wove my way through the paths I heard the clock tower ring out, and became aware of a funeral in progress nearby. I paused to listen, and to observe the manner of the mourners. Such a strange fascination lies in the sadness of others.

The priest was halfway through his eulogy, saying:

"It may be shallow or it may be deep, but the strongest man on God's great earth cannot hold it for long. Value it, dear friends, and remember how lucky you are to take it as you venture forth through your day."

I pressed on, not wishing to disturb the family in their grief.

What did the priest speak of?

THE MUSIC MAN

The streets of New York are a thronging mass of traders, shoppers, pickpockets, delivery boys, and businessmen, all conducting their daily affairs in their own particular garb. All have particular mannerisms to identify them, from the quick darting of the pickpocket's hand to the booming voice of the stall owner.

Musicians also frequent some streets, adorned with a variety of instruments. Those who linger long enough can often hear an eclectic array of lyrics circling through the murky air. Indeed, a few days ago on a stroll through one such street, my interest was piqued by a fragment of song floating on the wind:

"What am I, oh out I cry; I can be thrown but never caught, and lost but never bought?"

I continued on my way, observing the light fading over the buildings and the humming, weaving throng of people in front of me, a human hive of manic bees.

As I walked on, I wondered if the singer knew the answer to his own question. He had every right to.

What was the answer?

THE MESSAGE IN
THE NOTEBOOK

There are certain times when, in the process of examining the pieces of writing I have committed to paper, I stumble across text which, on first inspection, has no present meaning to me whatsoever. I am forced to venture back through my mind, in search of the subject matter which was preoccupying me at the time, and reconstruct my intentions.

Last week, when confined to my rooms by a prolonged hailstorm, I found one such scribbling. I appeared to have written:

Fqq ymfy bj xjj tw xjjr,
Nx gzy f iwjfr bnymns f iwjfr.

I eventually recalled that I had concealed some lines of poetry using a shift cipher, moving each letter forward a certain number of places within the alphabet.

How did the lines of poetry read?

BEWILDERING NOTES

As is often the way with writing, on some days my ideas flow as swift as a river, with no hope of regulating the flow. At other times, drought takes my thoughts, and what sentences remain seem to dance in a tarantella of dismay, blurring my paragraphs into an incoherent morass of words. In such times, morbidity and despair seep through the cracks in my adjectives, and I feel my work gain an air of wretched desolation which cannot be balanced by the development of a plot, or the fascination of the characters.

It is on days like these that I have become accustomed to organizing my notes and tidying my desk. These small things help me gain clarity in my creative vision upon my return. This is often an illuminating process in itself, yielding poems and paragraphs written in a midnight frenzy before being cast aside and abandoned as doggerel. These previously rejected scrawls can throw light on unrelated chapters. Such moments of clarity are rare but pleasing.

On one such organizational frenzy, I found some notes which I recalled I had written when thinking of settings for a short story.

Alas, I had roundly rejected them all, and torn the paper into shreds.
Yet I felt that I could reassemble the scraps, with a little effort.

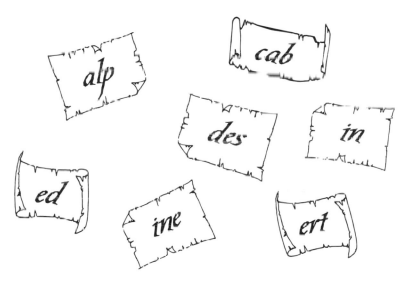

What short story setting had I been proposing?

THE AUDITORIUM

After a trip to the opera one evening, I found myself wandering through the dark alleyway at the side of the building, and on past the stage door. It lay ajar and, since no one was in sight, I pushed it open and entered the sacred rear of the building, into the world of actors and musicians, acrobats and dancers.

As I wandered among the glittering dance costumes and abandoned pots of paint, I was drawn to a closet from which a curious assortment of objects spilled. They seemed to be the props for a production set in a college, judging by the array of books and gowns which cluttered the alcove.

As my eyes grew accustomed to the gloom, I saw a prop which brought back memories of my own time at university.

This object, I recalled, always grew blacker and blacker each time it was cleaned, and yet whiter and whiter the more it was used.

What was this contrary item?

THE MATHEMATICAL TOME

I have a book of ancient mathematics in my possession, a volume which has long since languished unread, its knowledge in hibernation.

During a restless moment, I plucked it from its dormancy, intending to consult its classical wisdom. Yet as I leafed through the pages, strange markings swam into my vision—marginal notes from a previous owner, or perhaps of my own devising in a state of distracted, forgotten agitation.

1

11

21

1211

111221

I spent several hours trying to fathom their meaning, and my eyes had grown weak from studying the curves and corners of the figures before their meaning alighted in my weary brain and the next number in the sequence became clear.

What number should come next in the sequence?

NAMING DILEMMA

Finding names for one's characters is a strenuous task. Often the name which seems the most appropriate can sour in the mouth of the character as the story develops. I find villains especially challenging — crafting a name with a suitable edge of depravity can take a considerable amount of time.

While searching my notes for some befitting syllables with which to baptize my latest rogue, I stumbled across a series of words, all missing their connection. A single word can be fitted between each pair to create two entirely new words. One new word is formed by reading the first and central words together, the second by reading the central and second words together.

AFTER _ _ _ _ _ LESS
CUFF _ _ _ _ AGE
BRIM _ _ _ _ _ WARE

What were the missing words?

THE APPARITION

Last night I awoke to see my darling Virginia standing in the corner of the room. Her eyes gazed away from me, staring at the shadows of the world that lurked beyond the windowpane. I knew her to be an apparition, but as she stood there, the moonlight streaming around her, I saw her flesh prickle with the cold air and my heart fully believed her to be alive again.

As I struggled to bring myself to full consciousness, she turned, and I shrank back against the bed in horror. She was not my lost wife, but a vile wraith in uncanny disguise. Her eyes were sunken and burned with a terrible lust for fear. I knew not if I was dreaming, but when she spoke her words seemed to penetrate directly into my mind:

"I can prophesy your future, Edgar. All of your sorrows; all of the pain you will experience—I can predict."

The spirit glared defiantly into my eyes, but I started to wake and felt my courage growing, laughing at the spirit. "Why, vile spirit, I can prophesy the future too, with no less accuracy than you."

At this I slipped back into slumber, convinced of the certainty of my claim.

Why was I so sure?

THE SECRET
SOCIETY

The freemasons have long used cryptic gestures and elaborate ceremonies to draw together those who enter into the organization's circle, yet they are not the only group whose solemn rites are conveyed to a select few.

I heard once of a secret society in Boston, few in number yet great in name. Their headquarters were in an imposing building, with statues of Athena, Hera, and Artemis standing tall, gazing with probing eyes at any who progressed beyond the lofty grille of the gate.

I have an acquaintance who has passed through their halls, yet even with this connection I could not tell you much about their observances. The only information he has given me is this question, posed to new members:

"What am I, that I show up at the end of every weekday, and yet I only appear at the end of four months?"

What is the answer to the question?

A PROBLEM OF NUMBERS

As a writer I am naturally drawn to the delicate intricacies of language, and find immense satisfaction in creating linguistic conundrums, and yet there is also an intense beauty in mathematics and numerals.

A recent submission in response to my letter to the *Messenger* employed a fascinating mixture of the two arts:

January = 7 + 1
April = 5 + 4
November = 8 + 11
August = 6 + 8
June = 4 + 6
October = ? + ?

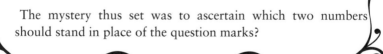

The mystery thus set was to ascertain which two numbers should stand in place of the question marks?

THE SHABBY GRAVEYARD

I sometimes linger outdoors as the first sigh of a storm scents the air with its musty breath, while others pull inside and batten their doors and windows, waiting for the squall to pass.

There is a certain excitement in watching the trees standing tall, resisting the swirling gales, and counting the minutes between the lightning strikes while listening to the crescendo of thunder in the sudden dark.

After the noise has abated and the world returned to stillness, I may walk out to observe the changes in landscape. On one such walk, I passed a wooden sign lying at the roadside, splintered into many pieces. It seemed to bear a name, and in my curiosity I gathered the fragments together, in an effort to discern who might have lost the item.

At length, I had pieced together the sign, which seemed to belong to a learned individual.

What was the name (and title) of the sign's owner?

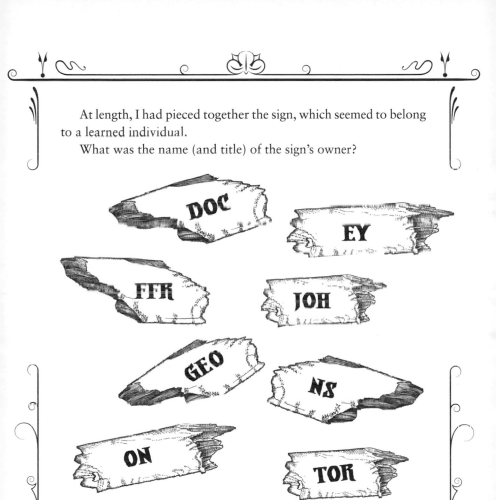

THE SLEEPING LADY

A letter arrived from the *Messenger*:

Dear Mr. Poe,

I hesitated to send you this week's submission as—given your prowess in poetry—I fear it will give you no challenge at all. Yet in the absence of any opposing offering, I have enclosed what I have.

Mr. Poe,

I have a strange tale for you, that of a lady who lies in eternal sleep, with dreams her only permanent company. A clock chimes outside her window once every day. My question for you is: at what time does the clock chime?

> *At the end of a sunless hall,*
> *The Lady Stella lies asleep,*
> *Mild as dawn she lies in repose,*
> *In slumber by the painted wall.*

Dare not rouse her from her dreams;
Never stir her from her rest.
In endless sleep she lies alone,
Gently drifting on conjured streams.

How long she will lie there none can tell;
Those who find her rarely dwell.

So—at what time *does* the clock chime?

THE LANDSCAPE OF
THE NIGHTMARE

I fear I shall forever be plagued with visions of gravestones and the swooping fiends of Hades. Once again my mind floated free from my body, denying me the peace of quiet darkness, and terrible scenes materialized behind my still-shut eyelids.

I found myself in a landscape walled on all sides with great volcanoes, their sides too steep and smooth for any to scale. Plumes of macabre smoke rose from their pinnacles, and great bubbles rose to the surface of pools of mud all around.

I cried out to whatever unholy figures might populate the wilderness and, to my surprise, a reply rang back to me. Yet my heart quickly sank back into desperation, for I recognized the voice—it was one which could repeat my thoughts with perfect clarity, and yet never share any of its own.

What was the voice?

A VISIT
TO THE CRYPT

My correspondence with an acquaintance in upstate New York led to the intriguing revelation that he had moved to a new property, an old stone building that held a crypt beneath the flagstones of its hall. I felt a curious draw to this sanctuary of graves and visited at his first convenience.

We entered the dim confines of the vault in uncanny silence, and I revelled in the coolness of the stone beneath my feet and the subtle dampness of the air.

After our eyes had become accustomed to the lugubrious gloom, my friend drew my attention to a most peculiar monument in the corner of the chamber: a single stone, overlooked by three statues of men in long robes, serious of expression. I held my candle to the stone to read the inscription which some long-ago craftsman had etched into it:

Here lie two fathers and their two sons; separated in life but united again in death.

I questioned my friend as to who the statues portrayed, and he replied that he believed they showed all of the fathers and sons referred to on the stone.

Assuming no statues had been removed, how could this have been?

FROM THE EDITOR 4: VOWEL RESTORATION

A letter arrived from the *Messenger*:

Dear Mr. Poe,
I am an avid reader of your work, and find the descriptions you employ in your short stories to be masterful. It is one of my great pleasures on a dark evening to return to your more morbid tales, and gaze out of the window into the night with the images you create echoing through my mind.

Inspired by your Messenger *appeal, I have assembled a collection of words all upon the same theme, and all of them brutally shorn of vowels. I trust some small entertainment will be provided as you seek to reinstate the missing letters.*

TRG
PPRTN
FR
LRM
BMNTN
NPLSNT
BHRRNC

Ever yours,
R.P. Whitemill

What words had the letter's author sought to conceal?

A MOURNFUL LETTER

This week's letters from the *Messenger* included a particularly eclectic selection of codes and ciphers. It was hardly an arduous task to ascertain the meaning of most of them, but I was struck by the doleful tone of one in particular:

Dear Mr. Poe,
I am a very old man, reaching the end of my time on this earth.
As I pen the final chapters of my existence, I find myself consumed
with regret at the mournful nature of life's end. Surely it is better
to return full circle, and embrace the playfulness of youth, in spirit
if not in body?

With this in mind, I have responded to your fascinating letter in
the Messenger *with a passage I hope will entertain you.*

> Utter no dark, elegiac remarks.
> At sunset, hold affection dear.
>
> Your friends instil righteous thoughts, relieving exhausted
> emotion.

So now tell me this: when my time is up, where will I be
buried?
Yours,
Z

What answer did I find to this melancholic question?

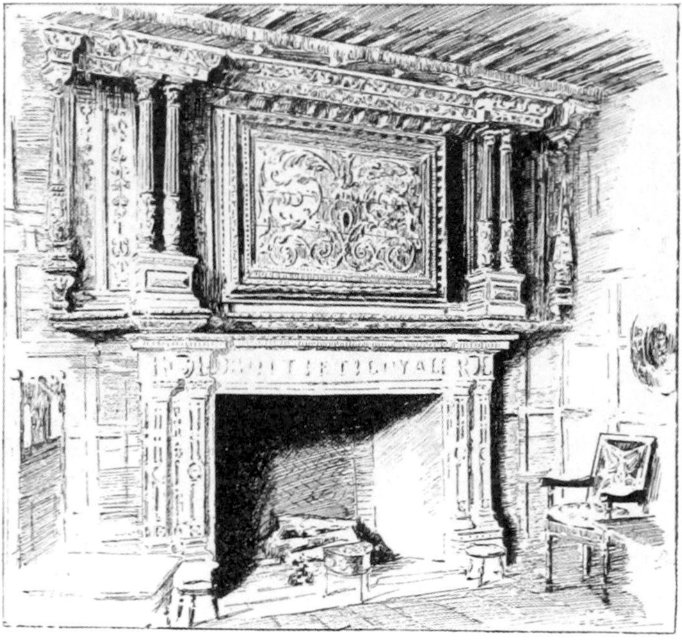

A SECRET ENTRANCE

I set out one afternoon on foot, to visit an acquaintance who had written to me not two days previously to invite me to his newly acquired property in one of the wealthier suburbs of Richmond.

As I progressed silently along the curve of the driveway, an ominous sense of foreboding sank upon me—the curling smoke issuing from the chimneys ahead wound around the brickwork like a shroud, concealing the architecture in an inscrutable film.

As soon as I arrived I was ushered into the darkness of the library, replete in its dark teak panels with intricate scenes of woodland creatures carved into them, their eyes glaring from behind winding branches. It felt as a house with a spirit of its own, reverberating from the very foundations.

On mentioning this to my host, he informed me of a mysterious clause in the deeds of the house. The document mentioned a secret chamber, which could only be opened in one way.

"Find that which flies swift as a bird, on wings of stolen feathers, bringing death with its beak."

I cast my eyes around the room, until finally they alit upon the object he described, carved into the panels above a particularly elaborate scene.

What was it?

THE NURSERY

I had ridden out early one morning to the house of an old acquaintance, a doctor of excellent reputation in the Baltimore area. He lived in a sparsely populated part of the town, studded with ancient plane trees.

After the purpose of my visit was complete, I took the opportunity to walk around his house, a fine architectural specimen with many hidden alcoves and corridors that stretched around corners into distant obscurity. At the end of one such corridor, I found myself in a room which must have been a nursery, some many years ago. A row of dolls sat on the windowsill, staring vacantly at distant clouds. A cracked toy box lay open on the floor, seemingly abandoned.

Everything in the room was covered in a thin layer of dust, except for a collection of carved wooden letters which stood on the desk. They stood incongruous, as if they had been recently handled, and held tall in a curious sequence:

S M H D W M Y

I noted that whomsoever had arranged these letters had done so with method, given their apposite nature.

What did the sequence represent?

FAMILY
MATHEMATICS

I was at the offices of the *Messenger* one afternoon, engrossed in a discussion of Mr. Longfellow's latest poem, when I heard two of the writers engaged at the newspaper deep in conversation about their families. It seemed that the course of their discussion had revealed some curious mathematical details.

The two men, named Albert and Edmund, were both married: Albert to Jane, and Edmund to Lucinda. They calculated that the ages of both men and both their wives led to a sum total of 133.

Not only this, but Edmund and Lucinda were the same age, yet Albert was double the age of Jane. Edmund in his turn was exactly 14 years younger than Albert.

How old did I deduce that Albert, Jane, Edmund, and Lucinda were?

THE HEN HOUSE

There is a farmer who is the proprietor of a small farmstead a few miles down the road from my own residence. I have been drawn to his estate on several occasions, as it is surrounded by trees with branches that twist into the most intriguing shapes, throwing sinister shadows over the damp ground.

There is a hen house at the edge of his estate; a fine home to chickens with the most lustrous black feathers you ever saw. I recently became aware that new hens had been introduced, of a speckled white variety with brilliant orange feet.

One day I came across the farmer cleaning the coop and, in the course of our conversation, it came to light—as you might suspect—that he had purchased the new chickens in order to increase his egg supply. It transpired that, on average, a group of four black and three speckled chickens produced as many eggs in six days as a group of three black and five speckled chickens produced in five days.

Assuming that all black chickens have the same egg-laying rate, and all speckled chickens have the same egg-laying rate, then which type of chicken produced more eggs, on average?

A WINTER WALK

In the sinister, unruffled silence of deep winter days, when the hedges are clasped by the bitter fingers of icicles, life seems to slow—even the birds' wings seem caught in water.

I progressed out on one such day, my feet cracking the mirrors of the frozen pools which had grown reflective plates in the dips of the road. The streets were empty, and as I passed through the great mouth of a bridge and into the body of the town, I saw but one other soul.

She seemed distracted as she walked, and seemingly incomprehensible utterances dripped from her lips like melting snow. Saving them from oblivion, I heard her say:

"Two in Maryland, North Carolina, and California; one in New Hampshire; yet none in New York or Illinois."

I did not linger in the biting cold, but cast a look over my shoulder as she walked away, considering her words.

What was the woman talking about?

THE MAN OF
MEDICINE

I once lived not far away from the residence of a most eminent
doctor, a specialist in the field of human digestion who had
studied at several of the best universities in the world.

He often related amusing anecdotes when we greeted each other in the street, and I became fond of his quiet, dry disposition.

He told me of a class he once led, with an obnoxious youth who assumed that his collection of wealthy relatives was qualification enough to enter into the illustrious profession. To quell the student's conceited entitlement, he would set them riddles unrelated to medicine—puzzles for which they had no grounding and were required to think laterally.

I told him that I would be keen to see such riddles myself one day, and in due course a folded piece of paper was pushed under my door. It contained no other text bar the following:

Which is the odd one out:
0, 8, H, N, R, S, or I?

Two digits and five letters, but no immediately discernible rule. Which was the odd one out?

THE AGE OF
WISDOM

The other day, I came across a letter I had once written to my wife. It read as follows:

My dear Virginia,
I am anxious to see you and be near you once again. Auntie has sent me word of your accomplishments, but it is nothing compared to hearing them for myself.

I have been busy writing my poetry, with occasional discursions into mysteries. I must say that this latter is starting to interest me more and more of late. Indeed, I shall now recount for you a strange event which I was recently led to by my work.

I had received a letter from my publisher requesting me to visit him when I could, and chose a warm but cloudy day to travel across to his large house on the outskirts of town. Upon my arrival, I was greeted by a pale-faced servant who led me through a warren of corridors. As we progressed

deeper into the gloom, we passed several rooms decorated as though for a child, although none could be heard—but then even our footsteps were swiftly consumed by the rich carpets.

In response to a query, the servant told me that the publisher had a son. He then proffered that, "The combined age of father and son is sixty-six, and—what is more—their two ages remain unchanged even with their digits reversed."

My darling, at first I thought this must mean that they were 11 and 55, or a rather less likely 22 and 44, but I have since thought of two further potential solutions as to the ages of the father and son.

Can you find them too?

Forever yours,

Edgar

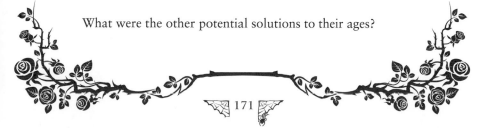

What were the other potential solutions to their ages?

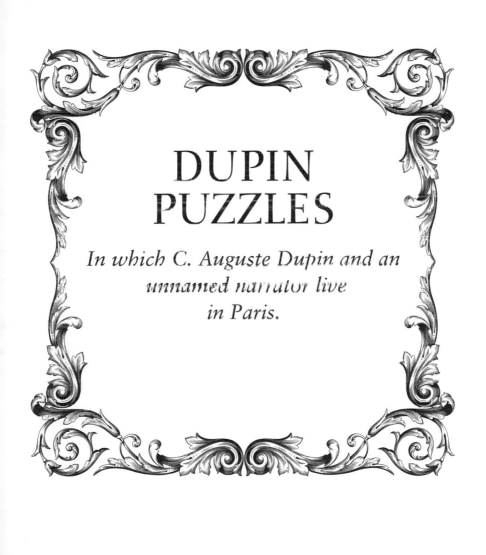

DUPIN
PUZZLES

In which C. Auguste Dupin and an unnamed narrator live in Paris.

INTRODUCTION

The man you are about to encounter in the following pages is an acquaintance of mine of some substantial intellect, the *chevalier* C. Auguste Dupin, whom I met through both happenstance and a shared propensity for delving into the dustier corners of libraries.

He is a character of mysterious origins—indeed to this very day I am hazy on the finer details of his life before our paths crossed in the heart of Paris, knowing only that untoward events had led him to an unostentatious existence in a somewhat austere abode in the XVIth *arrondissement*.

Despite his undisclosed troubles, the winding course of life has led him to be one of the most perceptive minds in the city, with a talent he employs to solve the most perplexing of crimes. Using his particular gift for ratiocination, he is a master of comprehending the criminal psyche. Indeed, our mutual acquaintance, G.—a member of the Paris constabulary—is now reliant on his expert talents to disentangle the webs of deception which descend to plague the city.

I have undertaken herein to recount some of the more bewildering cases we have faced, as well as a selection of riddles and enigmas with which Dupin has tested my powers of reasoning over the years. And now I invite you to test your own powers of ratiocination in divining their solutions.

THE
CHURCH CLOCK

I t was one of those days where the pace of time seemed to ebb and flow, like the tide on a phantasmagoric beach. Some hours rushed past in an anxious whir, the flow of people hastening along the arteries of the city, while others passed with a slow and sleepy gait.

There is a clock tower not far from the rooms in which Dupin and I reside, and the hourly chimes fall through our window to punctuate the day, whether desired or not. Sometimes, Dupin will stand by the curtain and look out at its ever-moving hands, amusing me with puzzles about the hours and minutes it describes.

"My friend, the afternoon is getting on… can you guess the time? How many minutes is it until three o'clock, if in six minutes' time it will be twice that same number of minutes past two o'clock?"

What time was it?

MURDEROUS INTENTIONS

One evening Dupin seemed in a more discursive mood than usual, and interrupted my contemplations on four separate occasions to inform me of his thoughts. I am not usually given to displays of annoyance as my

disposition is resolutely level-headed, but I must admit that after the fifth such interruption I was forced to speak my mind and redirect him to a more productive activity:

"Dupin, if you will insist on disturbing the peace of my evening, can you at least devise some form of puzzle through which I might occupy myself?"

My friend chuckled at my outburst, and sat in thought for some minutes before answering my request.

"Well, then let me tell you of a certain sight I witnessed a couple of evenings ago, while out working on a case.

"I saw a man wrap his hands around a neck, then twist with all his strength until I heard a loud pop And yet no one was injured."

What had Dupin witnessed?

IN THE
PERIODICALS

Paris is a gloomy city during those long weeks of January characterized by low-hanging mist and dark afternoons. Dupin and I entertain ourselves by reading various periodicals, and on one evening when we were both settled in such entertainment beside a small fire, he presented me with an amusing coincidence.

"My friend, it has just struck me that five words in the same article of this newspaper share a particular property.

"The words are as follows: 'wronged', 'spoon', 'tonic', 'polka', and 'unfed'."

"And what on earth is such an article about?" I replied in jest, while in truth setting my mind to the problem.

What was the solution I eventually found?

HIEROGLYPHICS 1

Dupin has always held a great fascination for the hieroglyphics of ancient Egypt, and is in the possession of many rare books which seek to discern their meaning. Indeed, he has become so enthused of late that he has begun to devise his own versions, with sequences of images enclosed in cartouches which represent words or expressions from the English language.

He recently presented me with one such cartouche:

"Ah, Dupin, have you been reading the sensational sections of the newspapers again?" I exclaimed, upon sighting this.

But what English phrase does his cartouche represent?

THE SHORT-SIGHTED BOATMAN

There are more than a few men who make their living on boats on the Seine, ferrying people across the dark, tumultuous depths, or transporting goods to the markets which line the squares of Paris.

An unfortunate number of Dupin's investigations took us to the banks of the river, and today a body had been found drifting next to one of the many walkways which follow the water's path.

We began to question one of the ferrymen who worked in this industrious stretch of the city.

"I barely saw the unfortunate man until he had almost drifted past me. I always say on days such as this, you see less and less when the more there is."

"I'm afraid I don't quite follow," I told him as Dupin looked at him with an unreadable expression. "More of what?"

What was the boatman referring to?

THE CODED DEATH

It has been some time now that I have lived in Paris with C. Auguste Dupin, a gentleman with an extraordinary capacity for ratiocination who has already solved several seemingly impregnable cases.

I arose one morning to find my good friend and companion pacing around the drawing room in a state of frenzied agitation. Upon querying as to the source of his anxiety, he recounted a chilling tale.

"Early this morning, I learned of the death of a man in a hotel in Saint Germain. His room was in a state of disarray, and among the wreckage of broken vases and torn curtains lay his corpse, his blood congealing on the carpet.

A message was scrawled on the calendar on the bureau near to where he lay, which read as follows:

Do not trust:
1 3 4 11 12 4

"The police cannot make head nor tail of this writing, but, my friend, I immediately gave them the name of a lady whom they should seek to question."

What conclusion had Dupin reached?

THE SUSPICIOUS GUEST

L ast night, over a supper of coq au vin, Dupin related to me the story of a most mysterious sequence of events he had become involved in some years previously, before we had made each other's acquaintance in the city of Paris.

Visiting the city of Lausanne, in Switzerland, he had taken up temporary residence in a small hotel in its ancient heart. While sitting at the window in that hotel's intricate lounge on the evening of his arrival, looking out into the gleaming eyes of the city, he became aware of a woman speaking to the manager with a look on her face of both puzzlement and distress.

Attuning his ears to their conversation, he had heard her relating to the manager that a man had knocked on her door and yet, when she answered, had apologized for disturbing her—for he had thought the room was his own.

The manager listened patiently and replied in the affirmative when she asked if the man was staying in the hotel alone.

What was the reason for the woman's unease, beyond any concern anyone might feel if any stranger knocked on their door in error?

THE AILUROPHILE

There is a woman who lives a short walk from the rooms I share with Dupin, a great cat lover whose animals can often be seen stalking the streets in search of mice. We are most grateful for their help, and I have grown quite in awe of their ability to pass through the night, silently vaulting the dark walls, unnoticed by all but the most observant.

Her cats have come and gone over time, and I often find myself at a loss when speaking to her as to how many cats she currently plays host to, and whether they are black, tabby, or otherwise decorated.

In our last conversation, she told me that all of her cats were ginger apart from two, all were white apart from two, and all were calico apart from two.

I pondered to myself on my way home as to the total number of cats in her possession, and found I had all the information I needed to deduce the solution.

How many cats lived in the woman's house?

ALL IN THE MIND

Dupin and I were sat at dinner one evening, contemplating the philosophy of imagination and the ability of the human mind to weave the supernatural out of the mundane fabric of life. Dupin looked up from his plate and spoke thus:

"Imagine that you are climbing down a mountain. Picture the light which had just a moment past bathed that snowy peak in pale gold, and then the evening cold creeping within your thin walking jacket.

"Your supplies are running thin, and as you scramble down the craggy path, a rockfall descends and blocks every route available to you. There is no way either up or down the mountain.

"Now, in this exact situation that I describe, what is the simplest thing you can do to safely settle your mind?"

NOTHING TO WORRY ABOUT

D upin and I were visiting a large property outside of Paris as part of an investigation into the disappearance of a young Montmartre man from his office.

The imposing front door, adorned by a knocker in the shape of a coiled snake, led onward into a corridor with rich crimson walls swirled with shapes too indistinct to easily discern by candlelight. As we moved silently through the house, I noticed Dupin become entranced by a small guest room, comparatively unadorned but still neatly arranged.

In the corner, next to a bow window, stood a writing desk covered with scraps of paper and scattered with pens. On one of the scraps was written an intriguing series of apparent equations:

$384 = 0$ $1,075 = 1$
$4,626 = 0$ $10,920 = 2$
$320,509 = 2$ $1,047,030 = 3$
$39,301 = ?$

Dupin raised the paper to the watery light filtering through the window panes.

"My friend, this will not help us find our quarry, but despite its extreme simplicity it is an amusing problem nevertheless. Can you ascertain what number should stand in place of the question mark?"

MEMBERS ONLY

During our many sojourns outside Paris, Dupin and I have encountered all kinds of people—from chevaliers through to chefs, and from artists to judges—and our aptitude for observation is now well-known. Although it is not our habit to venture outside of our abode more than necessary, one evening we found ourselves ensconced in the lodgings of a prominent mathematician, sharing a carafe of fine Bordeaux.

As the conversation drifted on, I found my attention wandering and so remained on its outskirts, considering instead the cascade of shadows pooling at the base of the candlesticks and curtains. Eventually, I was pulled from my reverie by a subtle increase in the animation of Dupin's voice.

"…the fascination of it is not the complexity of calculation but rather the multitudinous possibilities presented by various mathematical components. Do I understand you correctly?"

"Indeed," the mathematician quietly replied. "Dupin, may I present you with a small problem to illustrate?

"The smallest numbers hold unbounded potential, thus: eight eights can yield one thousand. How can this be?"

How indeed can eight eights be transformed into a total of one thousand?

THE STUDENT'S TALE

I was sat at my desk one afternoon, deeply engrossed in my volume of *Metamorphoses*, when Dupin returned with a puzzling tale.

He recounted that he had been walking along one of the wide avenues of central Paris when a tumble of students had hindered his path.

"They all seemed in high spirits, and were variously discussing geometry, trigonometry, and other such mathematical arts which today's youth are required to address in their classrooms. Intrigued as to the nature of their lesson, I stopped one of the young men and requested him to show me a problem he had encountered in the day's tuition."

"Without hesitation, he opened an exercise book, and showed me a page which read '8 + 8 = 91' "

"But Dupin", I exclaimed, "surely he must have been mistaken?"

"Not in the slightest," he replied, "for the equation was perfectly correct as written."

How is this so?

ROMANVS ✳ PVBLIVS EQVES OVIDIVS NASO

HIEROGLYPHICS 2

After another afternoon of poring over his hieroglyphics, Dupin presented me with another pictograph of his own invention, a series of images which together represent a word or phrase from the English language.

"Ah Dupin, what have you done now to get yourself into trouble?" was my only response.

What phrase did the cartouche represent?

STROLL IN PARIS

I find solace in the dusty silence which settles on the days I spend with Dupin; the way we grow into the dim corners of our Paris abode as if we were part of its very wood and stone. Despite this, when he does occasionally break the hallowed quiet with a spoken thought, I usually find myself intrigued by his musings. Just this afternoon, as we strolled the streets of Paris, he came out with one such meditation:

"Answer me this. What falsification can be constructed from both important eeriness and omnipresent satire?"

What answer did he intend?

THE BUSINESSMAN

After Dupin and I had successfully resolved another mysterious crime which the French police had been wholly unable to solve, I accompanied the enigmatic man into the central *arrondissements* of Paris to complete some necessary errands.

We paid a visit to an upholsterer to make a request about the refurbishment of a much-worn chair. Once a price had been negotiated, I observed Dupin casting his eyes over the dark mahogany wall panels whose waxy sheen was fading fast, and a broken window fastening through which an icy breeze was creeping.

"Are you falling upon hard times, Monsieur Dupont? Your establishment has always been gleaming with care, yet by the look of it your time and money have been short."

"Ah Monsieur Dupin," the upholsterer replied, "my business partner has another trade which he has resumed of late, and which has taken him away from the city. I am finding it difficult to keep up with the weight of maintenance on my own, and I am sorry to say that some repairs have been neglected."

"What trade is it that has so importunely taken him away?" queried Dupin.

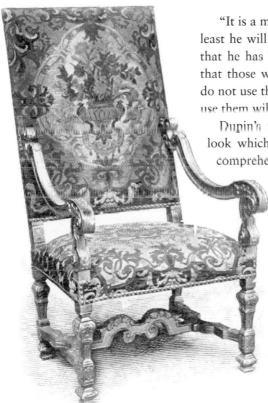

"It is a mysterious business, or at least he will not tell me directly. All that he has been willing to share is that those who buy his wares often do not use them; and that those who use them will never see them."

Dupin's face flickered with that look which I knew to indicate his comprehension. I later asked him of what the man had spoken. What do you think he told me?

A DAMP DILEMMA

At the end of a week of torrential rain, Dupin and I whiled away yet another evening with solitary reading in the peace and quiet of our Paris abode. Perhaps it was the nature of the weather, but a feeling of restlessness settled upon me which could not be shaken, and however hard I focused on the well-structured sentences of Voltaire, I could not quieten my mind.

At length, I decided to distract myself by devising a riddle for Dupin. His expert cogitation so often leaves me behind that the thought of successfully bamboozling him with a problem of my own devising was highly appealing.

I called to him across the room, saying, "My friend, I have just seen a man walking along the street in this foul and dismal deluge, without a hat or other wear upon his head, or an umbrella, coat, or overhang to shelter him, and yet there is not a wet hair upon his head.

"How can this be?"

Dupin looked at me with something approaching pity. Then, "I am afraid I do not even have to pause my thought to solve your little problem", and then immediately gave me the solution I was expecting.

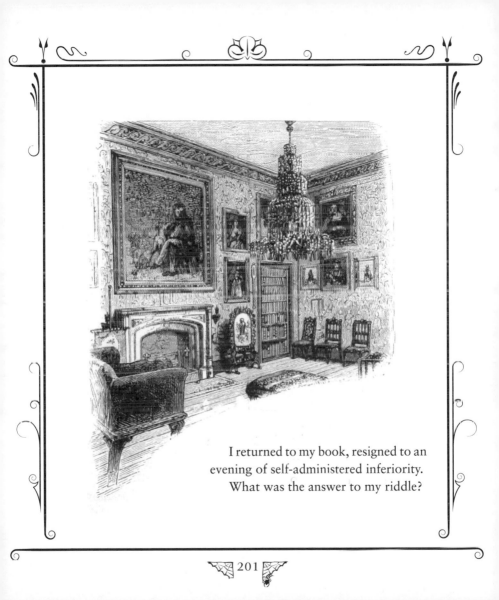

I returned to my book, resigned to an
evening of self-administered inferiority.
What was the answer to my riddle?

THE AGE OF DISCONTENT

The adventures that Dupin and I have tackled together in Paris have presented many harrowing situations, but none more perturbing than the murder scene of a young woman which we attended near the Palais de l'Elysée.

She had been found lying on a Persian carpet, in a pose that conveyed intense pain and distress. The blood had drained from her body into a pool on the floor, and stained the disarrayed furniture with streaks of red.

The most mysterious part of the case was the lack of information about her identity or age. Those who lived around her reported seeing her on her way to the market or sitting reading in her front window, but she had apparently never stopped to speak to anyone, so even her name had remained secret. We found no papers to identify her, and the only information that we gleaned was from a letter that lay on her desk, which she seemed to have been writing to her mother. One line in particular caught our attention:

> *I wish you well on your birthday, mother—but I am quite in denial about my age. Whenever anyone asks my age, I only tell them that in ten years I will be double the age I was twenty years ago.*

How old was the woman when she died?

THE ERUDITE POLICEMAN

One of our acquaintances in the Parisian police force had stopped at our residence to collect his notebook, which he had left at a crime scene Dupin and I had attended with him the previous day.

"Thank you for its safe return," said the policeman, "but I must say, I am loathe to return home this afternoon. My wife has begun to use such facetious language to describe my spending, despite our abstemious ways."

After the constable had taken his leave, Dupin turned to me with a thoughtful look resting upon his face.

"Our friend's choice of vocabulary was most interesting today. And indeed, tell me this: what do the words 'facetiously' and 'abstemious' both have in common?"

What was the answer to Dupin's question?

THE AGE
OF THE MASTER

The age of my friend C. Auguste Dupin has always been a source of some mystery to me. His skin appears smooth and youthful, yet his eyes are lined and regard the world with a great sagacity.

One day, as I accompanied my friend along the Champs-Élysées, I ventured to ask him about his date of birth.

He paused for a moment, and when he spoke his words hung in the frosty air, as cold as a February night:

"It is in truth a subject I avoid thinking of, as the manner of my birth and the narrative of my childhood are complex and melancholy.

"Indeed, my age is but a boat that carries me forward through the years, further from those events of my past.

"But I see you persist so I will tell you this: nine years ago, I was double the age my mother was three years before she came of age at twenty-one."

How old was my companion when he answered?

A WINTER PUZZLE

There was one winter where Paris stopped moving. Winter descended in a smooth, coherent mass, covering the streets with layers of snow, and gilding the buttresses of Notre Dame with icicles.

There was little hope of moving about the city as, even outside the door of our sheltered rooms, the snow was piled over 3 feet high. Better by far to remain indoors, watch the meditative descent of the snow, and listen to the arctic hush which descends on busy cities in such times.

One evening Dupin had a mischievous look on his face, and I guessed he had some trick to play on me. He held out his hand, which was curled in a fist around an object which was hidden from my view.

"Well, my friend," said Dupin, "as we are to be confined to these quarters for some time, I propose an activity for us. Perhaps you can guess what it is from my description of what lies concealed in my hand.

"Think of an object with edges that may fall in, jut out, or lie as straight as a rule, and which like the snowflakes

outside seems to never repeat the exact shape. You can place it wherever you like, and yet unlike the snow that so easily forms drifts, this object may only occupy one truly correct position."

Dupin smiled as he saw the confusion in my expression, and unfurled his fingers. What had he been hiding?

A MYSTERIOUS SEQUENCE

I try to avoid permitting my thoughts to linger on the more gruesome cases which Dupin and I have encountered over these years, as it is all too easy for the images of blood filtering from fatal wounds, and the empty gazes of sightless eyes, to overwhelm the necessities of the day.

Sometimes, however, such memories refuse to be stowed, and I often find my mind's eye returning to the pastel hues of an apartment in a building that stood overlooking the Louvre. This is the place where we found a young woman, slumped at the foot of her desk among a pile of papers, with a bullet wound darkening at the side of her head.

It was evident from the subject of the letters that she had been embroiled in some form of financial trouble and, in the process of combing through the woman's effects, the police had found folders full of complex, incomprehensible notes

which seemed designed to keep track of financial matters. One such note lay on the desk near the body, and a particular sequence had caught the investigating officer's eye:

F S T F F S S

Dupin considered it for a second before passing it to me. "What do you think this means, my friend?"

THE KEY TO THE PROBLEM

My existence in Paris with C. Auguste Dupin was one of acute solitude, beyond the company I shared with the great man. Books were constant companions, and the city yielded little else to divert us on a daily basis.

After a chance encounter at one of the many bookshops we frequented, a particularly valuable anthology of poetry came

into my possession, which I desired to send to an acquaintance in Orléans. However, I found myself in a quandary as to how to send it. I did not desire to send it unprotected in an unlocked container, and although I had a suitable lock for the container I decided that at no point was I willing to send my key through the postal system—even separately at a later date, for the key held great sentimental value.

I presented my dilemma to Dupin, who to my surprise, immediately summarized a neat solution that required no further equipment from me.

What was the solution?

HIEROGLYPHICS 3

Dupin had spent an afternoon out in Paris while I had remained in my quarters, distracted by a volume of Roman history I had recently acquired. When he returned, I was surprised to note that he carried a box, firmly sealed with a close-fitting lid and embossed with a gold symbol I did not recognize.

When I asked as to its contents, the only response I received was an enigmatic glance. However, later in the evening, as Dupin was once again engrossed in his hieroglyphic texts, a neatly folded piece of paper was placed in front of me.

"If you really want to know what I purchased today my friend, all you need to do is solve this pictograph."

What did Dupin's cartouche represent?

THE SUSPICIOUS GROUP

Most of the cases which Dupin and I have attended over the years have involved comparatively few people. Through pattern or chance, the deceased have largely lived alone, and only a select handful of friends and family appear to have broken into the orbit of their existence.

However, one case in particular involved a surprisingly large group. A death had occurred the evening prior to a scheduled dinner party in a strikingly large house in the Versailles district. Seven of eight overnighting guests had gathered in the library, to partake of a glass of sherry and admire the old volumes which stretched from floor to ceiling on mahogany shelves—but the final guest never joined them, and was later found dead in his room.

When questioning the guests, Dupin noted that without exception all of the guests seemed to think that an intruder was responsible. Indeed, a window had been broken in one of the ground-floor rooms so it seemed a likely explanation, yet Dupin seemed unconvinced.

I observed him kneel next to the window and run his hands carefully over the floor, looking intently for something. Other than for a dislodged book, the carpet was bare, and he finished

his search empty handed. He then walked out into the garden, where the shattered glass lay all over the ground, and seemed to inspect the window and its environs for some minutes before returning inside.

"I believe this crime was committed by someone in this house," he eventually declared.

What had Dupin been looking for on the carpet, and what did Dupin suspect?

A SOCIETY SCANDAL

Dupin is a man of some curiosity, and so whenever we have observed a crime scene on our walks through Paris we have inevitably altered our path in order to turn and study the investigations of the police.

One of these crime scenes I remember particularly vividly, as it turned out to be a society scandal which attracted the attention of the press, who of course delight in reporting on any unruly or disreputable habits of certain strata of Paris.

This particular event concerned a marquis, who had come into his fortune at a young age and made full use of his riches without ever concerning himself as to the impact of his actions. He had gained particular notoriety in the less salubrious areas of the city for gambling, since he had squandered a sum of money which to me was incomprehensibly large. As a result, he faced debtors at every street corner he traversed.

At such societal extremes, troubles have a habit of escalating fast, and it transpired that he had just been found dead on the ground in Montmartre, having fallen from some height. By chance we happened upon the scene mere moments after the tragic event, but already the attending police had—as is their propensity—assumed the death was self-inflicted, and that the young man had thrown himself from the tenth floor of the building where he resided, no doubt after the reality of his misdeeds had come crashing down upon his troubled mind.

While I was engaged in conversation with the gentleman in charge of police proceedings, Dupin quietly walked into the building and began to ascend the stairs. I cast my eyes up, and observed him opening a window on each floor, and looking down to where we stood below. After he had first opened and then closed the window on the tenth floor, he returned, and advised the constable to reconsider his opinion, especially given how calm the weather was today.

Why did Dupin suspect that the man had not taken his own life?

LILIES AND LILAC

Dupin and I had retired after dinner to read, and were comfortably settled in our customary places, illuminated by the familiar flicker of candlelight.

How many hours we have spent in such companionable silence! Yet, on this occasion, there was a different air about Dupin, and I sensed that something was on his mind.

At length, he relented to my questions and spoke to me of what preoccupied him. He spoke of a room filled with flowers: a cascade of lilies, marigolds, roses, and lilac which filled the air with wonderful fragrance. His words, so softly and fondly delivered, seemed to make the very air of our Paris apartment lighter, more fragrant with their descriptions.

"And yet," said Dupin, "although this is a room I will never lay eyes upon, I will nonetheless lie there one day."

What room is he referring to?

THE SUSPICIOUS PHYSICIST

Dupin and I were recently called to the laboratory of an eminent physicist, who had been found dead inside while working on an experiment to develop a new kind of compass. The scene was a curious one, for the door into the room had been locked from the inside, and had had to be broken through with an axe to gain entry.

There was just one window. Dupin walked over to it and noticed that it was fastened from the inside with a small iron bolt, running parallel to the bottom of the frame. A curious situation indeed. Yet, after opening the window, he noticed a scratch mark running along the wood on the outside of the frame, level with the bolt. At this, his eyes began to glow with comprehension.

"I think I know how the murderer escaped while leaving the door and window locked from the inside," he said.

What did Dupin suspect?

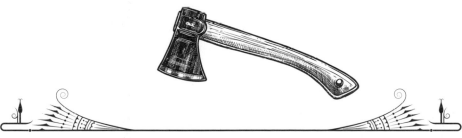

THE
FORTUNE TELLER

Dupin occasionally sinks into his own thoughts, descending to a place from which none can disturb him. When I see this mist fall upon him, I sometimes take myself to the Cirque Olympique, a remarkable building which hosts a spectacular variety of performers.

On my most recent visit, my eyes were drawn to a woman sat at a table covered by a silk cloth, decorated with swirling gold and purple. When she raised her head from the cards she appeared to be studying, I saw clearly that she was blind.

I approached her, and asked what she saw in her cards.

"I see many things, young man: omens of success and portents of despair. These tarot cards hold the future, if you know how to look. Come closer, and I shall teach you."

I approached and she showed me a particular trick, but so impressive was the feat that I felt sure she must be either not blind or must be using some kind of special cards.

Then, with a small amount of reluctance, I accepted a blindfold and placed it over my head. She then handed me her deck of cards, so I could try the trick myself.

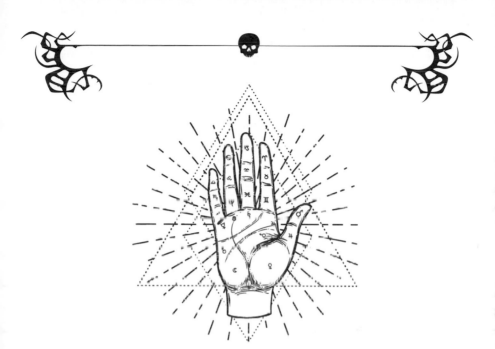

"There are seventy-eight cards in this deck I give you, and I have arranged them so that twenty are facing upward—the rest are facing downward. All you need to do is to separate the deck into two piles of cards, so that each has the same number of cards facing upward."

How could I do this, without removing my blindfold or looking at the cards in any way?

THE FISHMONGER'S PUZZLE

This year, the post-summer months have brought a certain calmness to the city of Paris, and Dupin and I have heard little from our acquaintances in the Parisian police. It seems there have been fewer cases than normal, and time has passed relatively undisturbed.

I have begun walking to the market in Saint Germain every morning in order to entertain myself. The characters one stumbles across on such a daily routine are astounding—it will always be a source of wonder to me how we humans cling to our ways no matter what.

There is one fishmonger who has begun to recognize me, and knows my trade. He seeks to challenge me whenever I pass, presenting me with a different pricing system for his stock each day. Yesterday he told me that it would be 5 francs for an eel, 7 for a trout, 10 for a halibut, and 16 for a langoustine.

"Ah Monsieur, but I will give you one of each for free if you can work out how I price my fish today!" he promised.

Can you work out what simple scheme the fishmonger had used to arrive at these values?

THE SUDDEN ASSAULT

A strong scent of baking led Dupin and I down one of the side streets of Paris' Latin quarter to a small patisserie. Though the lamps set into brackets on the walls were unlit and the premises seemed all but deserted, the smell was clearly emanating from within its walls.

The door was slightly ajar, and we tentatively entered, only to find a most pitiful sight. A young woman, covered in spots of flour, stood in the middle of the room, weeping next to a large hourglass which had evidently fallen from the countertop, and lay smashed upon the floor beside her.

"How am I ever to bake my pastry for the perfect amount of time?" the girl cried when she saw us standing in the doorway. "We have two spares upstairs, but they measure seven minutes and eleven minutes—yet this pastry needs to bake for fifteen minutes exactly."

Dupin raised his eyebrows, considering the problem, before announcing:

"You can achieve this easily enough."

How could it be done?

HIEROGLYPHICS 4

I was in the process of reading a piece of new writing which had been serialized in one of the more reputable newspapers, and over the course of my study had made some small exclamations to my companion Dupin about the strange conduct of one of the characters central to the narrative. It struck me as most odd that they should visit the places they did, let alone use the speech they chose to employ.

"Ah, but have you truly considered the intention of the author?", Dupin somewhat infuriatingly responded. "Do not judge them too harshly until the chronicle has reached its conclusion."

I muttered, largely to myself, that it was a mystery to me what technique the author could possibly be employing.

Dupin remained silent for some time, before handing me another one of his novel pictographs, once again wrapped up in a pseudo-Egyptian cartouche.

What does Dupin's latest pictograph represent?

THE WOMAN WHO WASN'T

Dupin and I had been resident in our remote abode for no more than a couple of months, with only each other's thoughts to amuse, when one evening he returned from a night-time perambulation with a conundrum for me.

I had spoken to no one for several days and was grateful of the diversion, so listened attentively to his voice as it echoed from that void that sat beyond the gloom that encased my candle's feeble light.

"I stopped this evening at Lapérouse to ease a hunger, but as I sipped my aperitif I observed a mysterious woman sat at the table opposing mine. She seemed in no hurry and was dining alone, but as I watched I saw a secretive smile creep across her face, until all her features were held firmly in its grasp.

"Intrigue overtook me, and I asked if I might join her. 'I'm afraid not', she told me, 'since I shot my husband earlier today, held him underwater, and then hung him—so he will be here to meet me any minute to witness the result.'

"After some moments of morbid confusion, her seemingly macabre tale suddenly made sense to me. Would you care to interpret her story as well, my friend?"

THE TIME OF DEATH

A message arriving from the Parisian police usually reports some form of unfortunate event, and just such a note last week led Dupin and I to leave early one morning to join the mysterious case of a librarian who had been found dead among the stacks of his medieval literature section.

As we progressed past the voluminous reference texts and works of literature, the scent of yellowing paper grew stronger, and we came upon the place where the body had been found. Despite the horror of the situation, I was immediately struck by a particularly beautiful clock which hung prominently on the wall above a desk

that sat at the end of the stack, decorated with a pattern of iridescent leaves and flowers.

While Dupin investigated the crime, I took a closer look at the clock, and soon realized that the time it displayed could not be correct.

"I despair of that clock," a stern-looking librarian said in response to my query, "for every time its hands cross over one another it loses three minutes, no matter how often I wind it up.

"I last reset it to the correct time yesterday, at 9:00 pm. And now, as you see, it is completely wrong."

Given the time right now is 9:40 am, what incorrect time is the clock showing?

THE STRANGE NUMBERING

In one of our occasional visits to the French countryside to investigate a case, Dupin and I found ourselves at a most imposing chateau, which was in the possession of a typically eccentric aristocrat. We had some hours to spare, so we decided to take a wander around the extensive grounds.

During our meanderings we came upon the stables and, having always had a fondness for horses, I opened the door to take a look. I was, however, most perplexed by what I found, and called Dupin over to see.

The stable blocks, whose labels were painted on the floor as below, were numbered in the most bewildering fashion:

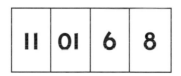

"Bewildering? Really?" Dupin commented to me. "Look again." What had I failed to notice?

THE AGES OF MYSTERY

I came across a strange, mathematical conundrum recently, which took even Dupin some time to solve, for at first sight it did not seem we were given sufficient information.

But I should start at the beginning.

There is an antiques shop on the corner of one of the small side streets of Montmartre which I have been known to frequent on quiet afternoons. Dupin has never accompanied me, and it is a source of some small pleasure to me to recount stories to him of the strange objects I have seen there.

It is a veritable maze of curios: roll-top desks are piled with dust-laden books, and lockets hang from the necks of wire-skirted mannequins. Taxidermy owls peer out of the gloom from the top of intricate glass-fronted cabinets, eyes forever wide.

The shopkeeper is a tall woman with a cadaverous face, raven-dark hair held back with a thick, velvet band, and an air of absolute certainty in her actions. On one of my recent visits, she told me in hushed tones of a story she had been told by a fellow patron of the establishment:

The customer in question was a census taker, who had visited a property to find the ages of its residents. A man standing at the door had told her, "We have three children, and the product of their three ages is thirty-six. The sum of their ages is the number on this door."

The census taker knew this was insufficient information to be certain of their three ages, and had therefore asked for more information. At this, the man had said, "I cannot speak any further—I must put my eldest to bed".

Content with this reply, the census taker had then left.

The shopkeeper asked me how this story could make sense, and I must admit I was equally perplexed. But Dupin was indeed able to work it out.

How old were the three children?

THE BROKEN GLOBE

In such disarray are so many of the crime scenes that Dupin and I attend. The violence which occurs before a death leaves a very particular chaos, one infused with the bleak uncertainty of who will sort through the items of the deceased, decide which objects are of enough worth to keep and which shall be cast away to the attics of auctioneers.

I remember vividly one such room, the study of a professor of history at the university, which had been found in a great state of turmoil, with the professor himself nowhere to be found. Suspicion had been aroused due to a great commotion which had been heard coming from his chambers.

As we picked through the carnage, I noticed a globe of astounding intricacy that had been cast upon the floor. I commented on its beauty to my companion but, as I rolled it over to look more closely, I noticed it had been marred by three large spots of ink, which had recently leaked from an ink jar that now sat above it, lying sadly on its side.

"An aside to this investigation, but this presents an interesting conundrum," said Dupin. "One could still display this carefully. What was the chance that these three spots of ink all landed on the same half of this globe?"

Assuming that the ink could have fallen at any three points on the globe, what is the literal answer to this question?

SOLUTIONS

SOLUTIONS

THE FITFUL REST
You could ask one of the women which vial the other would say is poisoned. In each case either the honest woman will truthfully report a lie, or the lying woman will lie about the answer from the truthful woman. In each instance you are told a lie, so you should take the opposite vial to the one recommended.

AN AMERICAN GARDEN
The letter "s".

A DIFFERENT TIME
The numbers here reflect the passage of hours on a clock, so 9 + 7 = 4.

A WRITER'S APHORISM
Each word is written backwards, so the message simply reads "what is poetry but mystery reflected?".

FROM THE EDITOR 1: THE HIDDEN TITLE
"The Arrow and the Song", which has been shifted forward 10 places and is a poem by Henry Wadsworth Longfellow.

THE DREAM
"You will hang me." This would be the truth if the executioner used the noose, meaning he should use the gun, and would be a lie if he used the gun, meaning he should use the noose. As this is neither directly the truth nor a lie, this third state might allow me to go free.

SOLUTIONS

SOLUTIONS

THE STATELY LETTER 30

Texas, Delaware, Ohio, Vermont, New York, Missouri, and Maine; the more recent additions to the Union, Idaho (1890) and Oregon (1859), can also be found: "The most exasperating aspect is how, amid a host of others, I can feel alone; without my own citadel, aware of how unsettled I am. Oh, I only know that over months of exploring I have once more gone too long without sufficient food; I am sinewy, or knifelike in profile. I miss our intellectual conversations, though mostly your domain, even when talking to others."

BOARDERS' ENTERTAINMENT 32

A river.

BIBLICAL WRITINGS 33

Each line consists of the letters of two names of a biblical pair (either people or cities) that have been muddled together, albeit without disturbing the order of the letters in the original names. They are:

ADAM and EVE
DAVID and GOLIATH
SODOM and GOMORRAH
SAMSON and DELILAH

THE SILENT BISHOP 34

The sequence represents the first letters of the first four books of the New Testament, Matthew, Mark, Luke, and John. The writer is saying that truth can be found in the four Gospels.

SOLUTIONS

To draw exactly one pint, Fortunato should fill the 3-pint carafe and
pour the contents into the 5-pint carafe. He should then refill the 3-pint
carafe, and once again pour into the 5-pint carafe until it is full. The liquid
remaining in the 3-pint carafe will then be one pint exactly.

It wasn't specified which guard had to face east and which west, so it was
possible for them to stand at opposite sides of the tower and face each other.

The letter "V", found in the words "convent" and "nave" but not
"kitchen".

A clock—an object with both a face and hands, but no fingers, eyes, or
mouth. The rhythmic beating came from the ticking of the clock.

Put the trousers on back to front. This will mean the left pocket will be
on the right side and the right pocket on the left, easily enabling one to
complete the challenge. Alternatively, the trousers could be put on inside
out, although it does make the pockets less accessible.

The missing words are, in order, AFTER, RUN, and POST, to make
HEREAFTER / AFTERWORD; OVERRUN / RUNAWAY; BEDPOST /
POSTMARK. Though there may be other possible solutions.

SOLUTIONS

SOLUTIONS

Twelve—for, after all, every month of the year has twenty-eight days (or more).

It would never be submerged. The ladder is attached to the boat, which will rise up along with any rising water.

Forty.

Because the growth we spoke of was my hair—and so he recommended a barber.

A deck of cards.

First, he could fill the 4-gallon cask from the 7-gallon, leaving 3 gallons in the 7-gallon cask. He could then fill the 3-gallon cask from the 4-gallon cask, leaving 1 gallon in the 4-gallon cask. After this, he could pour the sherry in the 3-gallon cask into the 7-gallon cask (giving 6 gallons) and empty the 1 gallon currently held in the 4-gallon cask into the 3-gallon cask. Then he could fill the 4-gallon cask from the 7-gallon, and fill the 3-gallon cask from the 4-gallon, leaving the correct quantities of 2 gallons (in the 7-gallon cask), 2 gallons (in the 4-gallon cask), and 3 gallons (in the 3-gallon flask).

SOLUTIONS

THE AVIARY
One cage contains 1,000 birds, another 400, and the final cage has 100. Were the largest cage to have ten times the number of birds of the medium-sized cage, as opposed to the smallest cage, then there would need to be a non-whole number of birds in each cage—which is clearly impossible.

FROM THE EDITOR 2
The French Riviera—every other letter has been deleted from the words in the letter.

THE BLESSING
The man was a Catholic priest, and so addressed by the title "Father".

THE BATHROOM
The man is a barber, and shaves other people.

THE HAUGHTY WOMAN
A locket, with a man's photograph inside.

TWO INTO FIVE AGAIN
In order, the missing words are CAP, SHIP, and WAY, making KNEECAP / CAPABLE; HARDSHIP / SHIPMATE; and ANYWAY / WAYLAYS.

NIGHTMARE IN THE STORM
Rain.

THE APOTHECARY
By filling the bottle with water, causing the feather to float to the surface.

SOLUTIONS

Lille, Paris, Nice, Nantes, Grenoble, Calais, Lyon, and Cannes:
"I write to you once again of my travels, this time to inform you that, since I fell ill, even I have taken up aristocratic tendencies in my old age. I now find it very nice to ride a fine white mare along the tracks of the French countryside, past the indignant estates of meagre nobles. The paths of the forest are musical aisles of birdsong, the thrushes singing sweetly on the boughs, I am reminded of the American nesting birds, although they lack their variety."

The "four" to take away from "seven" are the four outer letters, leaving the central "v", the Roman numeral for five. Similarly, if you take away the "two" outermost letters from the word "five" you are left with "iv", the Roman numeral for four.

"Are you sleeping?"

The letters are the first letter of the numbers from two onwards written as words, in ascending order starting from "Two". The next letter in the sequence would therefore be "E", the first letter of "Eight". Presumably the whole of the word "One" had already been erased.

The other end of the dog's rope was not tied to anything, so he could travel as far as he liked.

SOLUTIONS

A QUIET MOMENT
36. The brother would be 38 and the father 61, and 36 + 38 + 61 = 135.

THE MOURNERS
20. To reach the total of 70, 10 would visit on day one, 15 on day two, 20 on day three, and 25 on day four.

THE SPECTRAL SEA
He drowned. The clock times correspond to semaphore flag positions, which spell the word "DROWNED".

THE FLIGHT OF FANCY
"She choked". The answer is spelled out using the first letter of each bird named in the poem, taken in the order encountered.

THE CAT
The cat jumped from the ledge *into* the tower rather than *out of* it, falling only a short distance to the floor of the room.

THE GARDEN OF DEATH
He was a priest, and had married the woman to another man.

THE MENAGERIE OF DOOM
10 spiders and 9 beetles.

A CONCERTO OF MYSTERY
The message has been concealed by adding one extra letter to each pair, which in each case is earlier in the alphabet (or the same as) the correct letter. It reads: *The lead viola player is guilty.*

SOLUTIONS

"Meet me tomorrow at dusk". Each consecutive pair of letters has been swapped in the message, and the spaces have been removed.

The baby that the heavily pregnant woman was carrying—assuming that you count that baby as a person.

Siren, centaur, and manticore: "As I renounce my claim, I shall let the house fade into moonlight. I see It glow, bathed in the light of its pearlescent aura. I must complete this grim antic, or else I shall lose her love forever."

My shadow.

30 years old. In six years she will be 36 which is three times 12 (or 30 minus 18).

10 days. Comparing the maximum amount of lost time per day gives, for carriage v. grandfather clocks: Day 1 – 60s v. 1s; Day 2 – 120s v. 3s; Day 3 – 180s v. 7s; Day 4 – 240s v. 15; Day 5 – 300s v. 31s; Day 6 – 360s v. 63s; Day 7 – 420s v. 127s; Day 8 – 480s v. 255s; Day 9 – 540s v. 511s; Day 10 – 600s v. 1,023s.

SOLUTIONS

FLOWERS FOR THE DEAD
....108
14 days. On the 13th day there would be 91 blooms, and 105 on the 14th day.

AN EVENING OUT...110
Four. In the worst-case scenarios, after drawing three cufflinks I might have three different birds. No matter what, then, the fourth would have to match with one of them.

A VISITOR FROM THE SOUTH..111
The "visitor" in this case was a hurricane.

THE SIGN IN THE BREEZE...112
"STRANGER, ENTER AT YOUR PERIL". Each vowel has been replaced with the vowel which appears one vowel before it in the alphabet, with "A" being replaced by "U". The breaks between lines are also placed in the middle of words.

THE FAMILY HISTORIAN...114
Pennsylvania, Mississippi, Kentucky, New Jersey, and New Hampshire.

THE WRITER'S WAGES 116
The *Messenger*. $24 x 12 + ($1 + $2 + $3 + ... + $11) = $288 + $66 = $354.

A FURTHER LETTER FROM FANNY..................................117
In order, the missing words are "stature", "statue", "state", "sate", "sat", "at", and "a".

SOLUTIONS

SOLUTIONS

48 letters. On Monday there were 6 letters, then 10 were delivered on Tuesday, 14 on Wednesday, 18 on Thursday, and 22 on Friday for a total of 70 letters across the week. The total by the end of Thursday would therefore be 48.

TOGETHER, IN LIFE AND DEATH.

Breath.

Your voice.

The lines have been shifted forward five places in the alphabet. When decoded, they read:

All that we see or seem,
Is but a dream within a dream.

Rearranging the fragments reveals:

DESERTED ALPINE CABIN

A chalkboard.

SOLUTIONS

THE MATHEMATICAL TOME140

312211. The sequence is a "look and say" sequence, where each number is a representation of how the previous number would be read out if the sequence of digits was described aloud. The first line, "1", contains one one, so the next line is this first line explained in digits: 1 "1"s, i.e. "11". This then is two ones, so the next line is 2 "1"s, i.e. "21", and then so on.

NAMING DILEMMA141

In order, the missing words are TASTE, LINK, and STONE, making AFTERTASTE / TASTELESS; CUFFLINK / LINKAGE; and BRIMSTONE / STONEWARE.

THE APPARITION142

It may have been true that the spirit would predict the future, but so can anyone. The spirit did not say she would predict *correctly,* and nor did I claim to be able to

THE SECRET SOCIETY144

The letter "Y", found at the end of "Monday", "Tuesday", "Wednesday" etc. and "January", "February", "May", and "July".

A PROBLEM OF NUMBERS146

The first number in each sum represents the number of letters in the name of each month. The second number represents the numerical position in which the month stands in the calendar. Following this logic, the final line should read "October = 7 + 10".

SOLUTIONS

SOLUTIONS

Albert: 46, Jane: 23, Lucinda: 32, Edmund: 32.

Speckled chickens.

If "b" is the number of eggs a black chicken lays in a day, and "s" is the number a speckled chicken lays in a day, then $6 \times (4b + 3s) = 5 \times (3b + 5s)$. Expanded, this equation becomes $24b + 18s = 15b + 25s$, which is equivalent to $9b = 7s$ meaning that it takes 9 black chickens to produce the same number of eggs as 7 speckled chickens.

The letter "A".

"R" is the odd one out, as it does not have rotational symmetry.

Since there are two ages, if I reverse the digits in one and end up with the other age, then I am still able to meet the description given by the servant. So the other possible solutions are 51 and 15, and 42 and 24, which if reversed would become 15 and 51, or 24 and 42, respectively. You might also permit 60 and 06, were you to rather unusually write the age of 6 as "06".

SOLUTIONS

DUPIN PUZZLES

In which C. Auguste Dupin and an unnamed narrator live in Paris.

The time is 2.38 pm. The number in minutes until 3 pm is 22, and in six minutes' time, the time will be 2.44 pm; exactly two periods of 22 minutes past two o'clock.

A bottle being opened—Dupin had presumably visited a bar and seen a bottle being uncorked.

The letters in all five words are in reverse alphabetical order.

Head over heels.

Fog. The more of it there is, the less and less you see.

The code "4 3 4 11 12 4" corresponds to the first letter of months on the calendar. The fourth month is April, so the first, third and final letters of the coded word are all "A". The six numbers therefore decode to "AMANDA". Therefore Dupin recommended the police seek out someone known to the unfortunate man by the name of Amanda.

SOLUTIONS

If the hotel room had been the man's own, and he was staying there alone, he would not have needed to knock on the door—so he must have been lying.

Three—one ginger, one white, and one calico.

In this case, it is simply to stop imagining.

1. The numbers after each equality sign represent the number of zeros present in each number—as hinted at by the puzzle's title, "Nothing to Worry About".

The simplest solution is: $888 + 88 + 8 + 8 + 8 = 1,000$. Or a possible solution using only discrete "8"s is: $8(8 \times 8 + 8 \times 8) - 8 - 8 - 8$.

Dupin was looking at the page upside down, so the equation actually read "$16 = 8 + 8$".

Face the music.

"Misrepresentation". This is an anagram of both "important eeriness" and "omnipresent satire".

SOLUTIONS

THE BUSINESSMAN
The upholsterer's business partner had started making coffins.

A DAMP DILEMMA
The man was bald.

THE AGE OF DISCONTENT
Fifty.

THE ERUDITE POLICEMAN
Both words contain all five vowels in alphabetical order.

THE AGE OF THE MASTER
Dupin was 45. Nine years ago he was 36, making him twice (21 minus 3).

A WINTER PUZZLE
A piece of a jigsaw puzzle.

A MYSTERIOUS SEQUENCE
The sequence of letters are the first letters of the first seven ordinal numbers: first, second, third, fourth, fifth, sixth, and seventh.

THE KEY TO THE PROBLEM
I should send the container with the anthology inside, and with my fastened lock attached. The acquaintance should then attach their own lock and send the container back. I can then unlock and remove my original lock and return it to them, so the acquaintance can remove their own lock and at last open the container.

SOLUTIONS

HIEROGLYPHICS 3
Top hat—which is what he had bought.

THE SUSPICIOUS GROUP
If the window had been broken from the outside then it would have been unlikely for there to be no glass inside—instead, all the glass lay outside. Dupin had been looking for fragments of glass in the carpet.

A SOCIETY SCANDAL
Because if he had jumped out of the window it would have been open already, and Dupin would not have had to open it himself to look down. Being a calm day, it was unlikely the window had blown shut.

LILIES AND LILAC
The room where his future funeral was to be held.

THE SUSPICIOUS PHYSICIST
The murderer had escaped through the window, then used a powerful magnet to close the iron bolt of the window from the outside, causing the scratch mark level with the bolt.

THE FORTUNE TELLER
Count out 20 cards from the deck and then turn that pile upside down, while leaving the other remaining cards the original way up. And you are done! This works because if there are "n" upward-facing cards in the 20-card pile, there are 20 *minus* "n" cards in the remaining cards (since there are 20 upside down cards in the original deck). But if you then turn the first pile upside down, you have 20 *minus* "n" cards in the first pile too (since there are 20 cards in it in total). So both have the same number of upside down cards.

SOLUTIONS

THE FISHMONGER'S PUZZLE
Each vowel in the name of a fish is valued at 2 francs, and each consonant at 1 franc.

THE SUDDEN ASSAULT
Turn over both hourglasses, and wait for the 7-minute one to run out before starting to bake the pastries. The larger hourglass will then have 4 minutes left, so when this has elapsed you should turn over the large hourglass again to measure a further 11 minutes

HIEROGLYPHICS 4
Foreshadowing, since the cartouche shows "four [people] 'shadowing'". He is suggesting the writing style is foreshadowing future plot or character developments.

THE WOMAN WHO WASN'T
The woman had shot a photograph of her husband earlier in the day and held it underwater as part of the development process before hanging it.

THE TIME OF DEATH
10:16 am. A clock's hands overlap 11 times every 12 hours, so from 9:00 pm to 9:00 am they will have overlapped 11 times. If the clock was running to time they would not then have overlapped at all between 9:00 am and 9:40 am, but because it is running fast it will have already crossed again when it showed roughly 9:45 am. So the clock will be 12 × 3 = 36 minutes fast. Specifically, the hands overlapped at roughly 9:45 pm, 10:50 pm, 12:00 am, 1:05 am, 2:10 am, 3:15 am, 4:20 am, 5:25 am, 6:30 am, 7:35 am, and 8:40 am—and then again, because it is fast, at around 9:45 am.

SOLUTIONS

We were viewing the numbers upside down, and if viewed the right way up they in fact formed a simple sequence: 8, 9, 10, 11.

2, 2, and 9.

The product of the three ages is 36, and so there are only so many possibilities (assuming the ages are whole numbers, as ages are normally given). Now, the census taker herself *knew the sum of the ages* from the door number, but *this was not sufficient*—so the sum must have been one whereby there was more than one possible way of breaking it down into numbers that also multiplied to 36. What's then important is that discovering *there is an eldest child* resolves the ambiguity, so whatever those three ages are then one must be higher than all the rest (as opposed to having more than one child with the same, highest age).

If you work through the options, the only number that could have been on the door is 13 since this can be formed as both 1 + 6 + 6 *and* 2 + 2 + 9. All other possible products of three numbers equal to 36 have different sums of those numbers. But we know that there is an eldest, so the children must be aged 2, 2, and 9.

A certainty, as any sphere can always be rotated so that any three dots of ink will all appear on the same half.